M000158301

TREASURY OF
FLOWER LORE

Josephine Addison

illustrations by
Cherry Hillhouse

BLOOMSBURY

For my grandchildren:
Luke, Poppy and Kali

The creators of this work have made every effort to be
as accurate and up-to-date as possible.
The author and the publishers of this book
cannot be held liable for any errors and omissions.

All rights reserved: no part of this publication may be reproduced,
stored in a retrieval system, or transmitted in any form
or by any means, electronic, mechanical, photocopying or otherwise,
without the prior written permission of the publisher.

First published 1997 by Bloomsbury Publishing Plc,
38 Soho Square, London W1V 5DF

Copyright © Josephine Addison and Cherry Hillhouse 1997

The moral right of the author has been asserted

A copy of the CIP entry for this book is available from the British Library

ISBN 0 7475 2091 7

10 9 8 7 6 5 4 3 2 1

Designed by Neysa Moss
Typeset by Hewer Text Composition Services, Edinburgh
Printed in Hong Kong

INTRODUCTION

The significance and use of plants is so closely interwoven into the tapestry of our past that it must remain a mystery as to how and when it all began.

We know the ancient Greeks and Romans proffered them as symbols of victory, for endeavour, marriage, love, worship, as gifts and to heal the wounds of their warriors. Thus they became entwined in the mythology of their gods and as the Romans expanded their empire and invading armies colonized our islands, this rich variety of customs was gradually absorbed into our own pagan practice, with its own beliefs in witches, elves and fairies, charms and spells and ancient remedies, to which Christianity later added a further layer, quietly weaving strands around the original roots. They have almost faded away; however, I am delighted to say much remains of the old lore.

During the Tudor period the delightful language of flowers, whereby messages could be conveyed by the simple use of a flower or leaf, was well established and became a constant source of reference for poets and playwrights. The Elizabethan John Gerard (1545–1612), who was said to have more charm than integrity, published his famous *Herball or Historie of Plantes* (1597); it included a list of flowers growing in his garden, providing a useful chronicle of plants available at that time, although the book itself was said to contain many inaccuracies. The apothecary Nicholas Culpepper (1616–54) added to what was now a considerable wealth of information with his works, in which he prescribed herbs according to shape of the leaf, colour of the flower and habitat of the plant to the organs of the body suggesting cures and perhaps most extraordinary of all assigning trees and flowers to the various planets. This was a period of great expansion in the plant world as many species were being introduced, some having their own mysterious legends, names and remedies, adding to the already established country lore whereby many signs of nature were used to predict the weather, good and bad harvests, life and death and for the young at heart, love and happiness.

It was during the more romantic Victorian period that each day in the year was given a floral emblem bearing its own symbolism which was to be interpreted by the poets in verse and lovers in billets-doux.

Some plants in this book have a more interesting history than others and there are many with numerous country names, which for convenience I have limited to six for each flower, choosing those that are of particular interest.

And, as Margaret Brownlow wrote in her poem 'Tradition':

'In conclusion,
Linked by this scented rope that binds the centuries' fames
Lasting or quietly faithful, holders of all we inherit,
Come our own ages' herb-savants, privileged in those they succeed.'

Wildings of nature, or cultured with care,
Ye are beautiful, beautiful everywhere!
Gemming the woodland, the glen, and the glade,
Drinking the sunbeams or courting the shade;
Gilding the moorland and mountain afar,
Shining in glory in garden parterre
John Palmer 'Flowers'

ACONITE

Flower, that foretell'st a Spring thou ne'er
shalt see,
Yet smilest still upon thy wintry day,
Content with thy joy-giving destiny,
Nor envying fairer flowers their festal
May.
O golden-chaliced Aconite!
Thomas Noel 'The Aconite'

WINTER ACONITE (*Eranthis hyemalis*) The generic name is from Greek *er*, 'spring', and *anthos*, 'flower', referring to the early flowering of the plant, and latin: *hyemalis*, 'pertaining to winter'. Early botanists classified it variously as an aconite, a hellebore and finally as a ranunculus, which the Northamptonshire nature poet John Clare described as having

> . . . *buttercup like flowers that shut at night*
> *And green leaf frilling round their cups of gold.*

Its present name of *Eranthis* was given by John Hill, author of *The British Herbal*, in the mid-eighteenth century, who also referred to it as the 'flower of the earth' because of its short stem.

The winter aconite formerly carried a heavy burden for such a dainty flower by being identified with the classical aconite, a deadly poisonous herb dedicated to Hecate, the moon goddess of the witches in Greek mythology who retained her power under the rule of Zeus; she taught witchcraft and sorcery and was goddess of the dead – an unfortunate association for such a charming flower whose unusual petal and sepal formation is aptly described by Vita Sackville-West, in her poem 'The Garden':

> . . . *golden aconite,*
> *Dog Toby in his ruff, with varnish bright.*

Former names for the plant were the little yellow wolfsbane and winter wolfsbane, although it now bears the charming Lincolnshire country one of New Year's gift.

Winter aconite in the language of the flowers symbolizes lustre.

Early in the year drifts of the flowers mingle unobtrusively and naturally with grass, ornamenting woodlands, churchyards, the slopes of castles and country gardens, where the bulbs are often planted to complement the pure white of snowdrops, which the early gardeners recommended mixing together where they could be observed 'near windows or places of resort that their beauty may be seen'. With reference to the winter aconite, Henry Lyte (1529–1607), however, was less complimentary in his *Herbal*, stating that 'these venomous and naughtie herbs are found in this countrie planted in the garden of certain Herborists' while John Gerard noted a variation in the size of the flower according to the prevailing weather conditions when he wrote of them 'coming foorth of the ground in the dead time of winter, many times bearing the snowe upon the heades of his leaves and flowers; yea, the colder the weather is and the deeper the snowe is, the fairer and larger is the flower; and the warmer the weather is, the lesser is the flower, and woorse coloured'. During the early part of the nineteenth century the aconite was a popular pot plant in Paris in the home – a floral fashion that was to remain abroad.

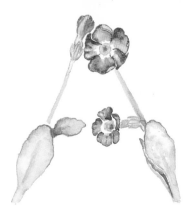

AURICULA

From the soft wing of vernal breezes shed
Anemones; auriculas enriched
With shining meal o'er all their velvet
leaves.
James Thomson 'The Seasons'

AURICULA (*Primula auricula*) The botanical name comes from Latin *primus*, 'first', and *auricula* is the diminitive of *auris*, 'ear'. It was formerly known as *Auricula ursi* or bear's ears from the shape of the leaves; they are also rather leathery and appear to be covered in a white meal, known as farina, which is in fact a waxy powder that can coat any part of the plant and explains the country name, dusty miller. It is also known as wild auricula, and is an Alpine flower known to the ancient Romans. The auricula is a descendant of a natural cross between *Primula auricula* and *Primula hirsuta*; the cultivars of today are the result of man's selection, in combination with a freak of nature giving the green-edge mutation to the petal, according to a recent article by Mary A. Robinson in the RHS journal, *The Garden.* The true wild one, however, is seldom seen in gardens today.

In 1597 John Gerard informed his readers that in the flower's native Switzerland the plant was a cure for vertigo, where mountaineers were advised that 'it preventeth the losse of their best joynts (I meane their neckes) if they take a root hereof before they ascend the rocks or other high places'.

The first auriculas are said to have been brought to England in 1570 by Flemish wool weavers who settled in Norwich, Ipswich, Middleton and Rochdale. Between 1620 and 1685 Huguenot refugees from northern

France and Belgium arrived, also bringing plants with them. They were accustomed to displaying the flowers in pots, in what are known as auricula theatres (open-fronted boxes, not very deep, with shelves inside on which to stage the plants), and auriculas were ideal for small gardens, and also screened unsightly walls. Although the use of potted plants generally was a part of seven-teeth and eighteenth century gardening it was not until 1717, in Richard Bradley's, *Improvements of Planting and Gardening*, that some practical advice was given on the staging of this flower. 'Set your Pots upon shelves, one above the other in such a part of the garden where Morning Sun may only come on them; as the Flowers are commonly cover'd with a sort of Dust which contributes in great measure to make them beautiful, some covering must be prepared for their Shelter against Rains which are apt to wash it away, and destroy their Colours.' A screen or curtain was often used to protect the flowers from the sun.

During the early part of the nineteenth century the auricula was a popular plant with the miners and silk weavers of Lancashire and Cheshire, areas where many of the Huguenots had originally settled. New varieties and colours were introduced, societies formed and exhibitions held; a copper kettle was usually awarded as a prize. Wealthier growers with large gardens became interested in what was now classed as a florist's flower and in 1873 the National Auricula Society was formed.

In the language of the flowers auricula signifies 'Wealth is not always happiness', and it is also a symbol of avarice.

BLACKBERRY

Thy fruit full well the schoolboy knows,
Wild bramble of the brake;
So put forth thy small white rose,
I love it for his sake.
Ebenezer Elliot 'To the Bramble Flower'

BLACKBERRY (*Rubus fruticosus*) Rubus is the old Roman name for the plant, derived from Latin *rubor*, 'redness', from the colour of many of the species; *fruticosus* means 'shrubby'. It is also known as bramble, from Old English *bræmbel* or *brymbyl*, 'prickly'.

Country names include bumble-kite, brummel, brameberry, bly and scaldhead, either from an eruption on the scalp of children through eating too much fruit – the underripe fruit being indigestible – or from the curative effects of the leaves and berries for the complaint.

Many country remedies relied on a spoken charm as an aid to a successful result. A cure for rheumatism and whooping cough required a bramble arch, preferably rooted at either end on land belonging to two different people, through which the afflicted person would then crawl, saying:

In bramble, out cough,
Here I leave the whooping cough.

Boils and blackheads could also be magically removed by creeping on all fours, three times from east to west, and if this was done 'good luck will follow, for the boils will soon die away after the ceremony'. Children could also be cured of various complaints by being passed through the arch nine times at sunrise on nine successive mornings. Blackberry leaves were used to treat burns and scalds, and an unusual combination of Christian and pagan practice, is to be found in a charm for burns. Nine blackberry leaves were dipped in holy water and applied to the afflicted area whilst repeating three times to each leaf:

> *There came three angels out of the east,*
> *One brought fire and two brought frost,*
> *Out fire, in frost,*
> *In the name of the Father, the Son and*
> *the Holy Ghost.*

Blackberry is the birthday flower for 19 July, and a symbol of envy, lowliness, pain, grief, wickedness, remorse, weariness, death, riches which destroy the soul, that which holds the rose and beauty of the soul from answering the call of the deity. It is an emblem of Christ and the Virgin Mary. The burning bush in which the angel of the Lord appeared to Moses was said to be a bramble bush.

In Scotland the superstitious believed that the Devil poisoned brambles on Old Holy Rood Day (26 September) and were warned:

> *Oh weans! Oh weans! the morn's the Fair*
> *Ye may na eat the berries mair*
> *This nicht the Deil gangs ower them a'*
> *To tough them with his pooshioned paw.*

Fortunately in England one had more time in which to pick blackberries before they had been spat or urinated upon – Michaelmas, 10 October in the old Julian calendar. English herbalists, thought every part of the plant useful, even the young shoots, which were used as a salad herb, and also helped to fasten loose teeth!

BLUEBELL

Like smoke held down by the frost
The bluebell wreathe in the wood.
Patric Dickinson 'The Bluebells'

BLUEBELL (*Hyacinthoides non-scripta*) Linnaeus first named the bluebell *Hyacinthus*, associating the flower with the hyacinth of the ancients, the flower of grief and mourning. In mythology, Hyacinthus was a charming youth loved by the gods Apollo and Zephyrus, but Hyacinthus preferred the sun god to the god of the west wind. In revenge, when Apollo was playing discus with the youth Zephyrus blew the quoit off course, killing Hyacinthus. Apollo, grief-stricken, raised from his blood a purple flower, on which the words *Ai, ai* (Alas, alas) were traced, so that his cry of woe would exist for ever on earth. As our native variety of hyacinth had no trace of these mystic characters older botanists named it *Hyacinthus non-scriptus*, 'not written on'. Camoëns' *Lusiads* relates in canto IX:

> *The hyacinth bewrays the doeful 'Ai',*
> *And culls the tribute of Apollo's sigh,*
> *Still on its bloom the mournful flower retains*
> *The lovely blue that dyed the stripling's veins.*

The bluebell was also known as wild hyacinth, jacinth, wood bells, auld man's bells, ring o'bells and culverkeys.

It is the birthday flower for 30 September and symbolizes solitude and regret. In country legend bluebells are fairy flowers, and it was believed that if a child picked them, alone, in a wood, it would never be seen again. A mysterious aura is said to surround the plant and the children's singing, ring game, 'In and out of the dusky bluebells', is alleged to be a fairy or magical song with sinister overtones. Nevertheless it is sad to see this beautiful flower torn from its roots and carelessly abandoned as the culprits trail their way home, as John Keats observed in his poem 'The Posy':

The spreading blue-bells; it may haply mourn
That such fair clusters should be rudely torn
From their fresh beds, and scattered thoughtlessly
By infant hands, left on the path to die.

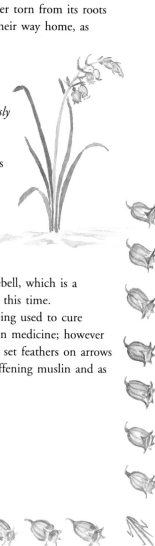

The flower is reputed to bloom on St George's Day, 23 April, and in former times blue was worn in celebration of the occasion.

On St George's Day, when blue is worn,
The blue Harebells in field adorn.

Older writers often confused bluebell and harebell, which is a summer flower and would not be in bloom at this time.

Although Tennyson speaks of the juice being used to cure snake bites the plant generally was little used in medicine; however in the Middle Ages the sap provided a glue to set feathers on arrows and the Elizabethans used it as a starch for stiffening muslin and as a paste for sticking paper.

BORAGE

And the Borage blue-eyed, with a thrill of
*   pride*
(For warm is her welcome on every side)
From Elf land coming to claim her place,
Gay garments of verdant velvet takes
All creased from the delicate travelling case.
Anon.

BORAGE (*Borago officinalis*) The common and generic names probably
come from Latin *burra*, a hairy garment, alluding to the downy leaves,
which give a distinctive flavour to summer wine cups and claret.

Here is sweet water, and borage for blending,
Comfort and courage to drink to your fill.

In the herbal of Apuleius it is referred to as corago and older writers
claimed that the name is a corruption of Latin *cor*, 'heart', and *ago*, used
figuratively to mean 'I rouse' because the plant was used to prepare
stimulating drinks; however, a further source suggests the name is derived
from *barrach*, a Celtic word meaning 'a man of courage'. The plant
named euphrosynon by the Greeks was probably borage; they put it in
their wine to give a feeling of 'being joyful and merry'. John Evelyn
(1664) records that sprigs of borage in wine 'are of known Vertue to
revive the Hypochondriac and chear the hard Student'. Therefore the
country name of herb of gladness seems most appropriate. Bees are
attracted to the bright blue star-shaped flowers, which may account for
another country name, bee bread.

According to Dioscorides, borage was the nepenthe of Homer which brought about forgetfulness and which Polydamna, wife of Thonis, sent to Helen for a token, with the unlikely claim that it was 'of such rare virtue that when taken steeped in wine, if wife and children, father and mother, brother and sister, and all thy dearest friends should die before thy face, thou could'st not grieve or shed a tear for them'.

Medicinally borage cordials were prescribed for long illnesses, palpitations of the heart, nursing mothers and consumption, therefore the quotation beneath the engraved frontispiece of Burton's *Anatomy of Melancholy* (1621) seems most appropriate:

> *Borage and Hellebore fill two scenes,*
> *Sovereign plants to purge the veins*
> *Of melancholy, and cheer the heart*
> *Of those black fumes which make it smart.*

Nevertheless, patients were warned of a possible overdose with drastic results – death.

In the language of the flowers it symbolizes bluntness and talent and astrologically is under the dominion of Jupiter and the zodiac sign Leo.

Formerly the fresh young leaves were used as a salad herb 'to ingender good bloud, especially in those that have been lately sicke', and the sky-blue flowers candied, by boiling them in a syrup of sugar and rosewater and strewing them with fine sugar before allowing them to dry, making a decorative sweetmeat. Borage is a good plant to have in the herb garden, both for its use as a herb and for the sake of its flowers, which yield an excellent honey, and the leaves and flowers can be added to cooling drinks giving a refreshing flavour of cucumber. A sprig of the plant cooked with soup and casseroles is said to improve the taste.

BROOM

Each spur and spire
A splendour outleaping, a flickering fire,
Thou wilt burn thyself out!
Why lavish thy gold
On this bleak hillside where no eyes behold?
Edward Thompson 'Wild Broom'

COMMON BROOM (*Cytisus scoparius*) *Cytisus* is derived from Greek *kytisos*, 'trefoil', in reference to the leaves of many species; it is said to be derived from Cythnos, an island in the Aegean, where some of the shrub like species abound. *Scoparius* is from Latin, *scopae*, 'a broom'. The common name is from Old English *brōm*. Country names include golden chain, green wood, basom and cat's peas.

This insignia of knighthood in heraldry was also the emblem of the Plantagenet family, whose coat of arms depicts a genet passing through two sprigs of broom. According to legend Geoffrey, Duke of Anjou, father of Henry II, saw the shrub growing amidst rock and poor soil prior to a battle. Plucking a yellow spray he fixed it in his helmet and thus adorned entered the battlefield, where the triumphant wearer was known by the *planta genista* (broom-plant) he bore. He is alleged to have said 'that golden plant ever be my cognizance, rooted firmly amid rocks and yet upholding that which is ready to fall. I will bear it in my crest, amid battlefields if need be, at tournaments, and when dispensing justice':

The chieftain who bore thee high in his crest,
And bequeath'd to his race thy simple name,
Long ages past has sunk to his rest,
And only survives in the role of thy fame.

In the language of the flowers broom symbolizes humility, neatness and servility and is astrologically under the dominion of Mars.

This 'memorial flower of a princely race' is surrounded by superstition. Some people regarded it as a magical plant of phallic significance, providing of course it was not picked during the month of May, the Roman month of death, when ill luck would befall the transgressor. There was a strong belief that:

If you sweep the house with a blossom'd broom
    in May,
You are sure to sweep the head of the house away.

A flowering bundle of broom decorated with ribbons was carried at country weddings as a symbol of good luck and the flowers along with other sweet-scented herbs were strewn along the bridal path.

Broom in full bloom was thought to be among the many signs for the departure of the cuckoo to a warmer climate:

Nor does she cease
Her changeless note, until the Broom, full blown,
Gives warning that her time for flight has come.

Older herbalists recommended the juice or a decoction of the young branches, or seed, for dropsy, gout and sciatica and to relieve the pain in the sides and swelling of the spleen, and the green sticks, heated in the fire, for toothache.

BRYONY

And a dead hawthorn stood upon the bank,
Whose branches summer yearly clothed
In pointed ruffles of lank bryony,
Rich in autumnal corals that the winds
Unclasp with difficulty from the boughs.
Revd Faber 'Sir Lancelot'

RED BRYONY (*Bryonia dioica*) The generic and common names are derived from the Greek *bryo*, 'to shoot or sprout', in reference to the vigorous growth of its annual stems; *dioica* refers to the dioecious character of the blossoms – flowers of a different sex appear on different plants. Apart from similar climbing characteristics it is unrelated to the black bryony.

Country names include wild nep, red-berried bryony, wild vine, wood vine and Our Lady's seal, as it has been the emblem of the Nativity of the Virgin since AD 695. From the large size of its pale, fleshy, forked tuberous roots, which were often suspended in herb shops crudely carved or trimmed to represent a phallus arose the name English mandrake; according to the *Universal Herbal* (1832) there was an alternative source of supply. 'The roots of Bryony grow to a vast size and have been formerly by imposters brought into human shape, carried about the country and shown for Mandrakes to the common people. The method these knaves practised was to open the earth round a young, thriving Bryony plant, being careful not to disturb the lower fibres of the root; to fix a mould, such as is used by those who make plaster figures, close to the root, then fill in the earth around the root, leaving it to grow to the shape of the mould, which is effected in one summer.' Bryony was sold as an aphrodisiac for humans and horses; it is said that male plants were taken by women and mares and female ones by men and stallions.

Naturally such a plant was useful in witchcraft. In *The Art of Simpling*, Coles tells us 'they make thereof an ugly image by which they represent the person on whom they intend to exercise their witchcraft'. This was accomplished in various ways, as the following lines suggest:

> *Witches which some murther do intend*
> *Doe make a picture and doe shoote at it;*
> *And in that part where they the picture hit,*
> *The partie's self doth languish to his end.*

The Romans had great faith in the plant as protection against lightning; Caesar Augustus favoured a wreath of bryony, which was placed on his head.

In the language of the flowers bryony symbolizes prosperity. Astrologically it is assigned to Mars.

During the fourteenth century the plant was used to treat leprosy and, later, the flowers for external and internal complaints; as Culpepper recommended, 'for stitches in the side, palsies, cramps and convulsions'. The juice from the stem was one of many wart remedies, and a decoction taken in wine, once a week before going to bed, allegedly cleansed the womb. Animals also benefited – one pound of the fresh root boiled in water was said to be the 'best purge for horned cattle' and a 'remedy for horse grip'.

ʽBUTTERCUP

The buttercups, bright eyed and bold,
Held up their chalices of gold
To catch the sunshine and the dew.
Julia Dorr 'Centenniel Poem'

MEADOW BUTTERCUP (*Ranunculus acris*) The generic name is from Latin *rana*, 'frog', because the numerous members of this genus are found in a similar habitat. *Acris* is derived from the Greek *akros*, meaning 'bitter'. All the members of the Ranunculus family have poisonous properties and tend to be avoided by grazing animals. This, however, did not prevent Irish farmers in the past rubbing their cows' udders with the flower of the buttercup on May Day in the mistaken belief that it increased the milk yield.

The buttercup has no perceptible fragrance but the glossy yellow hue of the expanded petals is an animating colour which helps to attract insects and children at play, who delight in placing the flower under a companion's chin to see whether 'they love butter' – a yellow reflection revealing the ones who do! – which gives credibility to the old country name of butter-flower. However, less attractive is the name crazy, as it was thought by some rural communities to be the 'insane herb' from the strange belief that the 'smell of the flower will make you mad'.
Batchelors' buttons is a name shared by many other plants, and there is also crowfoot. William Shakespeare's 'cuckoo-buds of yellow' are thought to be buttercups; the quotation, which includes other flowers of the field, comes from *Love's Labour's Lost*:

When daisies pied and Violets blue,
And Lady-smocks, all silver-white,
And Cuckoo-buds of yellow hue
Do paint the meadows with delight.

As buttercups and marsh marigolds
are found growing in similar habitats
they were given the strange name of
publicans and sinners. Marsh marigolds were also known as drunkards
– one assumes they must have been
the sinners. Nevertheless, it is the
daisy that is closely associated with the flower. For centuries the
quiet country pastime of making delicate chains of buttercups and
daisies in the meadows on a hot sunny day, has occupied and
amused children of all ages. Mary Howitt (1799–1888) wrote of the
flowers:

Buttercups and daisies,
Oh, the pretty flowers;
Come ere the Springtime,
To tell of sunny hours.

In the language of the flowers buttercup is the birthday flower for
18 September, symbolizing childishness, ingratitude, mockery, riches
and spite. In occult sciences it is a sun plant, supposedly acting
against stomach troubles and calming frantic or melancholy persons.

The juice of the buttercup applied to the nostrils is said to
'provoke sneezing and cure certain types of headaches' and the
leaves were used to produce blisters on the wrists in rheumatism,
and when infused in hot water as a stomach poultice.

CELANDINE

Mere idle followers of unthrifty May,
See in the lane, where geese and donkeys stray,
That golden flower, the countless Celandine:
Though long o'erlook'd, it needs no praise of mine.
Hartley Coleridge 'The Celandine and the Daisy'

LESSER CELANDINE (*Ranunculus ficaria*) The generic name is derived from Latin *rana*, 'frog', some species inhabiting marshy places, the habitat of the amphibian. The specific name is from Latin *ficus*, 'fig', an allusion to the shape of the tubers. Although it is a member of the buttercup family it has many more petals than the usual five, and is known as the lesser celandine to distinguish it from the greater celandine whose only link is in the colour of its flowers.

Country names for this early spring flower are figwort, smallwort, small celandine and pilewort, the latter arising from a long-standing cure for the relief of piles. An older writer observed that 'if you dig up the root of it you will perceive the perfect image of the disease commonly called piles'. An infusion of the plant, 1 oz. to a pint of boiling water taken in wineglass doses, was said to effect a cure in most cases; further relief was available in the form of an ointment consisting of the bruised herb and fresh lard, applied night and morning, which could be in the form of a poultice, fomentation or suppository. For the treatment of abscesses a preparation was made in early spring, when the flower is in bloom, which included elder-buds, houseleek and the leaves of the broad plantain. A recipe for a sore throat can be found in R. G. Alexander's *A Plain Plantain*, which advises: 'Take a pinte of white wine, A good handful of Sallendine, and boile them well together; put to eat A piece of

the best Roach Allome, sweeten it with English honey, and use it'.
The sap from the plant was used as a cure for warts and as the
flower is yellow it was used to treat jaundice.

The beauty of the celandine has made it a popular flower with
writers, the lakeland poet William Wordsworth in particular,
who wrote the poem 'To the Small Celandine', which
includes the sentiment:

> *Others, too, of lofty mien;*
> *They have done as wordlings do,*
> *Taken praise that should be thine,*
> *Little, humble Celandine!*

A carving of his favourite flower, of which
he had written

> *There's a flower that shall be mine,*
> *'Tis the little Celandine*

decorates his white marble tomb at Grasmere in Cumbria.

In the language of the flowers it carries the sentiment 'Joy's to
come', and is the birthday flower for 22 July. Astrologically it is
under the dominion of Mars.

For country people the flower was a weather oracle, closing its
petals before rain, although it seldom displays them before nine
o'clock and closes them by late afternoon. Wordsworth was aware of
this habit:

> *There is a Flower, the lesser Celandine,*
> *That shrinks, like many more, from cold and rain;*
> *And, the first moment that the sun may shine,*
> *Bright as the sun itself, 'tis out again!*

The superstitious carried the plant, with a mole's heart, as a
talisman against lawsuits and enemies.

CENTAURY

Pale Chlora shalt thou find,
Sun-loving Centaury,
Cranesbill and Sinjunwort,
Cinquefoil and Betony.
Robert Bridges 'The Idle Flowers'

COMMON CENTAURY (*Centaurium erythraea*). In classical legend the centaur Chiron, who healed wounds and taught mankind the use of medicinal herbs, cured himself with centaury of a wound he had accidentally received from an arrow, poisoned with the blood of the hydra – a water serpent with many heads.

There Centaury supplies the wholesome flame,
That from Thessalian Chiron takes it name.

The specific name is from the Greek *eruthros*, 'red', the colour of the flowers.

Country names include felwort, Christ's ladder and red centaury. The ancients named the plant *fel terrae*, earth gall or gall of the earth, from its extreme bitterness. As this bitterness was said to have a tonic and healing effect it was also known as feverwort and febrifuga.

In the language of the flowers centaury symbolizes delicacy and felicity and astrologically is under the sign of the sun.

Herbalists recommended that the whole plant should be collected in July, when the flowers are about to bloom, and dried. Centaury tea taken three or four times a day – one wineglass half an hour before meals – was said to be beneficial for those who were 'run down from want of appetite'. A cure for dyspepsia consisted of one ounce of leaves to one pint of water with barberry leaves added, which was also prescribed for jaundice and for kidney and bladder disorders. The virtues of a further decoction were many; if it was 'dropped into the ears, [it] cleanseth them from worms, cleanseth foul ulcers and spreading scabs of the head, and taketh away all freckles, spots and marks on the skin, being washed with it'. Powdered centaury taken in wine was alleged to cure the bite of an adder and the juice of the herb with a little honey added was 'good to clear the eyes from dimness, mist, and clouds that hinder the sight'. Healing and tonic effects generally were attributed to the plant although Culpepper advised: ''Tis very wholesome, but not very toothsome'.

It was considered a lucky plant by some of the Celtic tribes of Europe, although the more superstitious believed that if you put centaury under someone's nose 'he will run away as fast as his legs can carry him'. One ancient scholar claimed 'magicians assure us this herb has a singular virtue for if it is mixed with the blood of a female lapwing or plover, and put with oil in a lamp, all that compass it about shall believe themselves to be witches'. An equally exciting claim from a further source suggests 'those present will see themselves upside-down with their feet in the air'.

Centaury was widely grown during the Middle Ages and is still used today to flavour vermouth and other bitter herb liqueurs.

CHAMOMILE

With open velvet butterflies
That swung and spread their peacock eyes
As if they cared no more to rise
From off their beds of camomile.
Jean Ingelow 'Scholar and Carpenter'

CHAMOMILE (*Chamaemelum nobile*) The specific name refers to the value of the herb in medicine. The generic and common names are also Greek in origin and are derived from Greek *khamaimelon'*, 'earth-apple'. Chamomile was the Saxon *maythen* and with fennel, plantain, watercress, nettle, crab-apple and chervil was one of the sacred herbs of that period. In the past, chamomile had a reputation as the plant's physician as it was said that nothing contributed more to the health of a plant than to have the herb placed around the garden and that nine times out of ten, if a plant was drooping, the chamomile would revive it. When walked on the strong aromatic scent of the plant will often reveal its presence before it is seen, and it was often planted for this reason in the green walks in gardens and as lawns during the Tudor period; an experience which was said 'to delight the mind, and bring health to the body'. Unfortunately such lawns are rare today, although one can still be found in the gardens of Buckingham Palace. Nevertheless an old adage survives the mystery of time:

Like a camomile bed –
The more it is trodden
The more it will spread.

In William Shakespeare's *Henry IV part 1*, Falstaff uses the plant to make a moral judgement: 'though the Camomile, the more it is trodden on, the faster it grows, yet youth, the more it is wasted, the sooner it wears', and a further reference to the herb is found in *The More the Merrier* (1608):

> *The Camomile shall teach thee patience*
> *Which riseth best when trodden most upon.*

Chamomile is the birthday flower for 17 December, symbolizing energy in adversity, and love in austerity. Astrologically it is assigned to the sun.

Formerly no plant was better known to country people for domestic remedies, so much so that old herbals agreed 'that it was lost time and labour to describe it'. Familiar though it may have been the medicinal virtues were to be found in the fully expanded flowers, with their white-ray petals and conical yellow centre. Muslin bags stuffed full of chamomile flowers scented baths; steeped in water, they were said to reduce facial swellings caused by abscesses. The flowers were also used for chamomile tea, an extremely useful sedative and remedy for nightmares. The author Beatrix Potter was obviously aware of its effects when one of her characters, Peter Rabbit, was given chamomile tea to soothe him after his unfortunate adventure in Mr McGregor's garden. The whole herb was used in the manufacture of beer. William Browne, however, writing in *Britannia's Pastorals* (1613–16), had an alternative idea – he recommended its use with fish:

> *Another from her banks in sheer good will,*
> *Brings nutriment for fish, the camomile.*

CHICORY

Celestial blue the Chicory wheels
Speak of high Summer's picnic peace;
One hour it left the Hand that heals
For traitor's shame that shall not cease.
Margaret Brownlow 'Passover Herbs'

CHICORY (*Cichorium intybus*) The generic name is from the Latin word *cichoreum*, 'chicory', itself an adaption of the Greek *kichorion*, again the word for 'chicory'. *Intybus* is from *intibum*, the Latin for 'endive', *C. endiva*, which is an allied but foreign species, however, it was an old name for chicory.

It is also known as blue chicory, succory, wild succory and hendibeh. It has been suggested that the name succory comes from the Latin *succurere*, 'to run under', from the depth the root system seeks water. Tusser wrote of it:

White endive and succory, with spinage,
All such, with good pot herbs, should follow the plough.

A species of chicory is believed by some writers to have been among the 'bitter herbs' which God commanded the Israelites to eat with lamb, when the Passover was instituted.

According to legend Succory was a beautiful maiden pursued by the sun. She refused his advances and was changed into the plant destined to have its face uplifted towards him during the course of the day.

Linnaeus used the chicory as one of the flowers in his floral clock at Uppsala, because of its regularity in opening at 5 a.m. and closing at 10 a.m. However, the difference in the latitude would mean that it opened between six and seven in the morning and closed by noon in England, and obviously, was a familiar sign in rural lore:

> *On upland slopes the shepherds mark*
> *The hour when, to the dial true,*
> *Cichorium, to the soaring lark,*
> *Lifts her soft eyes serenely blue.*

Because of the flower's response to the sun's rays, it was believed by sympathetic magic that the water distilled from the flowers would improve fading eyesight. However certain precautions were necessary when gathering the plant – it had to be removed with a piece of gold or stag's horn, a version of the disc-shaped gold sickle which was used in ritual to represent sunlight, warmth and fertility. The most auspicious days for picking the plant were St Peter's Day (27 June) and St James's Day (25 July), although if the unfortunate gatherer should speak during his labours he would die. The superstitious believed that just holding the herb would make them invisible and that the leaf, in common with several other plants', would open locked doors if held against the lock. It is said to have been grown as an aphrodisiac but details of its efficacy have proved elusive.

The old herbalists used a poultice of the bruised leaves of 'this jovial plant' for swellings, inflammations and 'when boiled in broth for those that have hot, feeble and weak stomaches doe strengthen the same'. When infused, chicory gives a bitter taste to coffee and darkens the colour.

COLUMBINE

Gentle Lady Columbine,
What witching grace is thine.
Slender branches hung anon
With a flowery carillon.
Fretted leaves beneath thee spread,
Horned cap upon thy head.
Hoel Caerlion 'To a Columbine'

COLUMBINE (*Aquilegia vulgaris*) The generic name is from Latin *aquila*, 'an eagle', the flower spur resembling an eagle's claw, and the English name columbine from Latin *columba*, 'a dove' – the form of the flower suggesting a group of doves.

White doves brooding in the sun
(Thus the ancient legend runs)
There as in a quiet nest,
Happy thoughts may fitly rest.

A much older name is culverwort, from the Saxon *culfre*, meaning 'pigeon' and *wort*, 'plant'. Columbine is also known as doves in the ark, granny's bonnets, skull caps, fool's caps, aquilegia and ackely.

In the Christian tradition it is dedicated to Christ and the Holy Ghost, and is depicted with seven petals instead of the usual five, to typify the gifts of the Holy Spirit: counsel, knowledge, fear, piety, strength, understanding and wisdom.

It is the birthday flower for 1 April and signifies desertion, constancy and folly. In former times it was, like the willow, an insignia of a deserted lover, as we discover in a couplet from Browne's *Britannia's Pastorals* (1613–16):

> *The Columbine by lonely wand'rer taken,*
> *Is there ascribed to such as are forsaken;*

or as it is confirmed elsewhere:

> *The Columbine, in tawny often taken,*
> *Is then ascrib'd to such as are forsaken.*

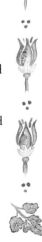

This long-time favourite of the cottage garden was described by John Parkinson, a seventeenth-century writer, as 'being carefully nursed up in our gardens for the delight of its forme and colours'. However, in *All Fools* by George Chapman (1605) the flower was less welcome, probably because it was seen by some as an emblem of cuckoldom.

> *What's that – a Columbine?*
> *No! that thankless flower grows not in my garden.*

As a popular garden flower, the columbine was represented in heraldry and was one of the badges for the House of Lancaster. 'It occurs in the crest of the old Barons Grey of Vitten, as may be seen in the garter coat of William Grey of Vitten (Camden Society, 1847), and is thus described in the painter's bill for the ceremonial of the funeral of William, Lord Grey of Vitten: 'Item, his creste with the favron, or, sette on a lefte-hand glove, argent, out thereof issuyinge, caste over threade, a braunch of Collobyns, blue, the stalk vert'.

Herbalists prescribed columbine seeds for measles, jaundice and smallpox, although the botanist Linnaeus warned of its dangerous properties; nevertheless, taken in wine it ensured a speedy delivery in childbirth. A lotion concocted from the leaves was recommended for sore throats and mouth ulcers.

COMFREY

King-cup and Fleur-de-lys
Upon the marsh to meet
With Comfrey, Watermint,
Loose-strife and Meadowsweet.
Robert Bridges 'The Idle Flowers'

COMMON COMFREY (*Symphytum officinale*) The generic name is from Greek *sympho*, 'to make to grow together', from its supposed properties as a salve for healing fractures. The common name is a corruption of *conferva*, which has a similar meaning. The plant was named and used two thousand years ago by Dioscorides, who Margaret Brownlow describes in her poem 'Tradition':

> *In the army of Nero the Ruthless a herb healer served,*
> *Dioscorides, laden with learning. His lore still connects*
> *With materia medica.*

It is said to have been brought to England by the Crusaders, who discovered its value as a healing agent. The monks grew the plant in their herb gardens where they were used to treat not only the wounds of the brothers in their infirmaries but also those of travellers and the poor of the community.

The country names of the comfrey often reflect its medicinal use as a salve for fractures: knitbone, nipbone, boneset and consolida; others include church bells, suckers and Abraham, Isaac and Jacob, the latter from the variation of the colour of the pink and white flowers which Henry Lyte described in his *Herbal* of 1578: 'The floures bee round and hollow like little bells'. Like other members of the borage family it has rough hairy stalks and rough long leaves.

According to the apothecary Culpepper, astrologically comfrey is under the dominion of Saturn and the sign of Capricorn, which suggests it is cold, dry and earthy in quality. He recommended that 'the roots being outwardly applied, cure fresh wounds and cuts immediately, being bruised and laid thereto; and is special good for ruptures and broken bones. Also, that if the root was spread on leather it would ease gout, painful joints and ulcers. In the book *Speculum Mundi* the plant is highly commended for curing wounds, also 'the slimie substance of the root made in a posset of ale, and given to be drunk, cureth the pain the back gotten by any violent motion as wrastling and the like; to which some add the overmuch use of Venus'.

Herbalists applied the fresh leaves to sprains and suspected fractures in the belief that reducing the swelling united the bones. An alternative method was to pound the root into a mucilaginous mass, drain the pulp through a linen cloth and pack it around the limb, previously washed in juice from the plant, which was then laid in a wooden trough splint. Michael Drayton recommended comfrey for lung complaints:

Campana here he crops, approved and wonderous good;
As comfrey unto him that's spitting blood.

The former poet laureate, Alfred, Lord Tennyson, using an older name for the plant, refers to its use as a modern remedy:

This, the Consound,
Whereby the lungs are eased of their grief.

CORNFLOWER

Now, gentle flower I pray thee tell
If my love loves and loves me well;
So may the fall of the morning dew
Keep the sun from fading thy tender blue.
Now I number the leaves for my lot –
He loves not, he loves me – he loves me not.
An old love charm

CORNFLOWER (*Centaurea cyanus*) The generic name is from the classical name of a plant of ancient Greece which is said to have healed a wound in the foot of Chiron, one of the race of centaurs, who had the head, arms and torso of a man, and the body and legs of a horse; *cyanus* refers to the distinctive blue of the flower. In Roman mythology, Cyanus was a youthful devotee of the goddess Flora, who wove garlands of flowers for her festivals. On his early death she transformed him into a cornflower, his favourite bloom, and one of the many flowers that lay scattered around him when he died.

Country names include corn blue-bottle, bluet, blue-bow, blue cap, bachelor's buttons and hurtsickle, the latter name from the plant's reputation for blunting the sickles formerly used to harvest the corn.

A treach'rous guest, destruction though dost bring
To th' inhospitable field where thou dost spring,
Thou blunt'st the very reaper's sickle, and so
In life and death becom'st the farmer's foe.

Nevertheless, children favoured this dainty flower, stringing the outer florets with a needle and thread and, having secured the ends of the

cotton, placing the colourful circlet between the pages of
a book – a charming keepsake which also retained its
colour. It is for this reason also that the petals are often used
for pot-pourri and the flowers dried for collage work. The
blue of the florets was popular with artists, who would
pound the fresh petals and use the residue as a pigment.

Unfortunately the cornflower, which was an abundant
wild flower, is now quite rare, although there are
garden varieties whose ancestors were cultivated in Tudor
times which were, according to John Parkinson in his
Paradisi in Sole, 'wholly blew, or white, or blush, or of a sad
or light purple, or of a light or dead red, or of an overworne
purple colour, or else mixed of these colours'.

In the language of the flowers cornflower signifies delicacy, and
a dweller in heavenly places. Astrologically it is assigned to Libra
and is under the dominion of Saturn.

Formerly the flower was used as a love oracle. If it was carried
in the pocket of a young man and survived, he would marry his
current sweetheart, but if it died, so would their love and she would
marry somebody else.

A water distilled from the the petals of the flower was a remedy
for weak eyes, and the famous French eyewash 'Eau de
Casselunettes' was made from them. The herbalist Thomas
Culpepper advised that 'powdered or dried leaves of the Blue-bottle
is given with good success to those who are bruised by a fall or have
a broken vein inwardly'. The fresh leaves taken in wine were a
plague remedy and the juice of the plant placed on fresh wounds
ensured rapid healing.

COWSLIP

Cowslips, sweetlips, smelling of summer,
Coming with the cuckoo, bringing in
the May,
Lifting heads in pastures, where the
cattle spare you,
Waiting to be gathered when the
children come to play.
Stephen L. Gwynn 'Cowslips'

COWSLIP (*Primula veris*) The generic name is a form of the Latin *primus*, 'first'; *veris* refers to spring. The origin of the name cowslip is obscure; according to one source it is simply a polite form of cow-pat. However it has been suggested that it is a corruption of cow's leek, leek being derived from the Anglo-Saxon word *leac*, meaning 'a plant'.

All the leaves of the cowslip form a rosette from which the stalk, crowned with delicate, tubular-shaped flowers, hanging on separate stalks, forms a fragrant umbrella. The many unusual country names of the cowslip include herb Peter and key flower, the pendant flowers suggesting a bunch of keys, the emblem of the apostle St Peter; in Norse mythology the flower was dedicated to the goddess Freyja, the goddess of sexual desire and was thought to admit her to her treasure palace. Naturally with a change of religion to Christianity the flower was dedicated to the Virgin Mary and became Our Lady's Keys and Key of Heaven. Petty mullein was also used as it was thought to be of that species, also fairy cups and paigle – which gave rise to the saying 'As blake [yellow] as a paigle'.

Astrologically the cowslip is under the sign of Venus. It is the birthday flower for 22 September, symbolizing pensiveness, winning grace, rusticity and comeliness, and in the language of the flowers it means, 'You are my divinity'. William Shakespeare mentioned the flower frequently in his work. In *A Midsummer Night's Dream*, he compared the upright cowslip to Queen Elizabeth's splendidly dressed Pensioners:

The cowslips tall her pensioners be.
In their gold coats spots you see;
Those be rubies, fairy favours;
In those freckles live their savours.

Picking cowslips by the basketful was a delightful summer pastime for children whose favourite flower it was, and they would often string fifty or so open flower-heads together by stretching twine between two chairs, then tying off the ends to form a fragrant, soft ball, known as a tosty. John Clare in his *Shepherd's Calendar* refers to this rural custom:

And cowslip cucking balls to toss
Above the garlands swinging hight
Hang in the soft eves sober light
These maid and child did yearly pull
By many a folded apron full.

Welsh girls would use the tosty as a love oracle throwing it from one to another, calling out the names of possible suitors:

Titsy tosty, tell me true
Who shall I be married to.

Adults favoured cowslip wine, which has a pleasant flavour and had an excellent reputation as a sedative. The fresh flowers were added to bathwater with refreshing consequences.

CROWN IMPERIAL

bold oxlips, and
The crown imperial; lilies of all kinds,
The flower-de-luce being one.
William Shakespeare *The Winter's Tale*

CROWN IMPERIAL (*Fritillaria imperialis*) The generic name is from Latin, *fritillus*, 'dice box', refering to the chequerboard markings on some of the species. A native of Persia, it was introduced to Vienna by Clusius in 1576 as the Persian lily and reached England some years later. The flower, which has been described as 'the lily of the turbaned countries' is said to have received its name from Alphonsus Pancius, physician to the Duke of Florence, because it was grown for the first time in the Imperial Gardens of Vienna. However, it does have another but more unfortunate name, stink lily, because the root smells, it is alleged, like a fox. Several famous gardeners commented on the odour; John Parkinson in his *Paradisus Terrestris* (1629), while devoting two pages to praising its beauty above all other lilies, notes that 'the whole plant and every part thereof, as well rootes, as leaves and flowers doe smell somewhat strong, as it were the sauour of a foxe'. This did not deter others with culinary interests: 'the roots of the Crown Imperial have a very nauseous smell' said one, 'yet are frequently stewed in soups, without yielding any noxious quality to the liquor, perceivable in the quantity used; but this does not by any means prove that they may be generally eaten with safety'. The roots are, in fact, poisonous raw but harmless when cooked.

Crown imperial is the birthday flower for 13 January and signifies majesty and power.

There are two kinds of this handsome plant, both bearing a circle of pendulous bright-coloured flowers – one a deep orange and the other lemon yellow, with a splendid crown of green foliage. Christian legend, however, suggests another shade; according to the story the crown imperial was formerly white, but during the Agony of Our Lord in the Garden of Gethsemane it was the only flower which did not bow its head and since that time blushingly hangs it in shame, with tears of repentance in its eyes – the nectaries at the base of the petals.

An old Persian legend suggests the tears are those of a queen whose fidelity was questioned by her husband. She was changed by an angel into the flower and until they are reunited the glistening drops will remain.

Early writers were fascinated by the nectaries, and John Gerard wrote of them: 'In the bottom of each of these bels there is placed six drops of most cleare shining sweet water, it taste like sugar, resembling in shew faire orient pearles; the which drops if you take away, there do immediately appeare the like, notwithstanding if they may be suffered to stand still in the floure according to its owne nature, they will never fall away, no not even if you strike the plant until it be broken'.

Since the flower was introduced it has been dedicated to St Edward, the tenth-century king and martyr who was murdered by his stepmother while drinking a stirrup cup. Superstition alleges it flowers on his feast day, 18 March.

DAISY

There, in thy scanty mantle clad,
Thy snawie bosom sun-ward spread
Thou liftst thy unassuming head
In humble guise
Robert Burns 'To A Mountain Daisy'

DAISY (*Bellis perennis*) The generic name is from Latin *bellus*, 'pretty' or 'charming', though an alternative source claims that it is *bellum*, 'war' because 'it is fitted to heal wounds in war'. Early physicians and apothecaries named it *Consolida minor*, because it was said to heal wounds. Daisy is a corruption of day's eye, from the Old English *dæges eage*, so called because it is said to close its pink lashes and go to sleep when the sun sets, as Chaucer comments:

> *Well by reason men it call maie*
> *The Daisie, or els the Eye of the Daie.*
> *The Empresse and floure of floures all.*

Country names include day's eye, miss modesty, white frills, bairnwort, little star and twelve disciples. Another old country name for the plant, measure of love, suggests its use as a love oracle. Today, girls still pick the petals off the flower, saying alternately 'He loves me' and 'He loves me not', the last petal revealing the answer. Another form of love divination was for a young girl to pick a bunch of daisies with her eyes closed, the number of flowers indicating the years before she married. A daisy root placed under the pillow would ensure dreams of a loved one.

It is the flower of St Margaret, whose feast is held on 20 July; she is

the patron saint of King's Lynn and on the Corporation seal is
represented as standing on a dragon and wounding it with a cross.
The flower was dedicated to her by the monks many years
ago.

   Daisy is the floral representation for the month
of July and is the birthday flower for 17 April,
symbolizing virginity, adoration and innocence.
In the language of the flowers it suggests 'I
share your sentiments'. A double daisy
signifies 'I partake of your sentiments', a
particoloured one, beauty, and a red daisy,
unconsciousness. In the Christian tradition
it is an emblem of Christ and the Virgin
Mary.

   Superstition surrounds the flowering of
the daisy and if you fail to tread lightly on the first daisy you see in
the spring, daisies will grow over your grave or that of your loved
one before the year has ended. It is said that spring is here when
you can cover three daisies with your foot although some sources
suggest seven or even nine. The root of the plant worn or carried
about one's person was a powerful charm against accidents or
illness. The roots were also believed to stunt growth, a superstition
which probably sprang from the idea that everything had the power
to bestow its own personality on others.

   Herbalists used the plant for syrups, oils, ointments and
plasters, a distillation of the flower as a liver tonic and the leaves to
reduce swelling of the testicles.

DANDELION

*Dear common flower, that grow'st beside the
  way,*
Fringing the dusty road with harmless gold,
First pledge of blithesome May
'Which children pluck, and, full of pride, behold,
High-hearted buccaneers . . .
J. R. Lowell 'The Dandelion'

DANDELION (*Taraxacum*) The generic name is a corruption of a
Persian word meaning bitter pot-herb. However an earlier interpretation
suggests it was derived from two Greek words; *taraxis*, 'inflammation of
the eyes', and *akeomai*, 'to cure', for it appears that the milky content of
the stalk was used for such a complaint. The name dandelion derives
from Middle English *dent de lyoun*, from French *dent-de-lion*, 'lion's
tooth', an allusion to the jagged, toothlike edges of the leaves.

Some of the country names of the plant are associated with its
reputation as a diuretic – piss-a-bed, swine's smart, pismire and wet-a-bed –
and until recent times it was widely believed that to smell the flower would
cause bedwetting. The plant does have stimulating elements that would
affect the bladder and kidney. Clock-flower, tell-time and what-o'clock
allude to a favourite pastime of children who love to blow off the downy
seed-heads, scattering them to the winds, counting each puff until the 'time'
is revealed. The poet William Howitt referred to this very old custom:

Dandelion, with globe of down
The schoolboy's clock in every town
Which the truants puffs amain,
To conjure lost hours back again.

Lovers also took advantage of this prophetic plant to test the depth of their sweetheart's feelings. If all the seeds blew away in one puff the blower was loved passionately; a few seeds remaining was a sign of some unfaithfulness; many seeds, indifference.

The resulting seed-head, bereft of its plumes, was known as priest's crown, which the poet James Hurdis aptly compares in his poem 'The Village Curate':

> . . . Dandelion this,
> A college youth that flashes for a day
> All gold; anon he dofts his gaudy suit,
> Touch'd by the magic hand of some
>   grave Bishop
> And all at once, by some commutation
>   strange,
> Becomes a Reverend Divine.

The dandelion is assigned to Leo and the planet Venus. It is the birthday flower for 27 September, symbolic of grief, coquetry and bitterness. As a bitter herb it is symbol of Christ's Passion.

Dandelion is a herb of great antiquity which is mentioned in the Bible and in the works of Dioscorides, Hippocrates and Theophrastus. John Evelyn, founder of the Royal Society, wrote 'Macerated in several Waters, to extract the bitternes, Dandelion, tho' somewhat opening, is very wholesome, and little inferior to Succory, Endive, etc.' In England today it is sadly neglected as a salad herb, although in parts of Europe, particularly France, it is very popular. The root of the plant is gathered in the autumn, gently roasted until golden brown, ground, and used as a coffee which is reputed to act as a sedative.

DEADLY
NIGHTSHADE

Trample not on a virgin flower!
I am the maid of the midnight hour;
I bear sweet sleep
To those who weep
And lie on their eyelids dark and deep.
Barry Cornwall 'The Night-Shade'

DEADLY NIGHTSHADE (*Atropa belladonna*) In Greek mythology Atropos was the eldest of the Three Fates and bearer of the shears which cut the Thread of Life of mortal beings without regard to age, sex or quality – an allusion to the poisonous qualities of the plant. *Belladonna* is the old name for the plant, derived from the Italian meaning 'beautiful lady'. One source suggests the reason for this was that ladies formerly touched their eyes with the plant or used a few drops of its juice to make their pupils large and lustrous and thus enhance their beauty; however another old writer promoted a different explanation – that it was used by an Italian, Leucota, to poison beautiful women; and a further derivation is founded on an old tradition that priests used to drink an infusion of the plant before they worshipped and invoked the aid of Bellona, a Roman goddess of war.

According to legends the plant belonged to the Devil, who tended the deadly nightshade. He was only diverted from his labours once a year, when he is preparing for Walpurgis night, the witches' sabbath on the eve of May Day. Therefore those who wished to gather the plant had to make unusual preparations – a black hen was released as a diversion because the Devil would not be able to resist chasing it, leaving the collector free to pick the protected plant, which explains other country names of Devil's cherry and Devil's herb.

Yet a further one, dwale, derived from the Scandinavian, was said to be William Shakespeare's 'insane root that takes the reason prisoner'. Earlier, the plant was used in sleeping draughts, and Chaucer alludes to the fact with 'There needeth him no dwale'; and Thomas Lupton (1585) wrote of it being an early anaesthetic, 'Dwale makes one to sleep while he is cut or burnt by cauterizing'. In contrast, the country name fair lady refers to the Greek goddess and enchantress Hecate, who presided over the lower world. It was supposed to have grown in her garden, one of nineteen herbs cultivated for potions and charms, whose qualities she taught to her daughters. Consequently all plants of a poisonous nature were sacred to her, some of which are mentioned by Ben Jonson in *The Masque of Queens* (1609):

And I ha' been plucking plants among
Hemlock, Henbane, Adder's tongue,
Nightshade, Moonwort, Libbard's-bane
And twice by the dogs was like to be ta'en.

Therefore it is not surprising that deadly nightshade bears the sentiment fateful gift. It is the birthday flower for 15 July symbolizing loneliness and silence.

Herbalists used the plant to treat a variety of complaints including rheumatism, gout, neuralgia, paralysis and nervous disorders.

DOG ROSE

We know the dog-rose, flinging free
Whip-lashes in the hedgerow, starred
*   with pale*
Shell blossoms as a Canterbury Tale,
The candied English genius, fresh and pink
As Chaucer made us think,
Singing of adolescent meads in May.
Vita Sackville-West 'Summer'

DOG-ROSE (*Rosa canina*) The specific name, *canina*, 'dog', is probably based on the Greek name for the flower, *kynorhodon*, because it was alleged to cure the bite of mad dogs; the Romans named it *canina*. A further explanation is that the flower was originally dag-rose – dag being a dagger – because of the thorns, and became changed because people did not understand the allusion. Nevertheless the prefix dog was occasionally added to the name of a flower suggesting it was worthless, maybe because of the lack of scent; another example is dog-violet. The actual number of roses indigenous to Great Britain is open to dispute by botanists, but there are five distinct species, each with their delicate colour, wreathing the hedgerows in sadly less profusion now, during the early summer months – burnet, downy, sweet briar, field and dog-rose. Robert Herrick drew a simple moral from the wild rose in 'To the Virgins, to Make Much of Time':

Gather ye rosebuds while ye may,
Old time is still a flying;
And this same flower that smiles today
Tomorrow will be dying.

Canker-rose is an old and distinctly unflattering country name for this favourite flower, which expresses contempt for its size and faint perfume in comparison to the garden varieties.

> The rose looks fair, but fairer we
>   it deem
> For that sweet odour which doth in it
>   live.
> The canker blooms have full as deep a dye
> As the perfumed tincture of the roses,
> Hang on such thorns, and play as wantonly
> When summer's breath their masked buds discloses;
> But for their virtue only is their show
> They live unwoo'ed and unrespected fade,
> Die to themselves.

The colourful scarlet fruit or hip (from Anglo-Saxon *hiope*) is generally described as flask-shaped and was highly recommended by John Gerard, assuring his readers 'the fruit when it is ripe maketh the most pleasant meats and banketting dishes as tartes and such like' commending them 'to the cunning cooke and teethe to eat them in the rich man's mouth'. Another old writer, whilst confirming their culinary use, wrote 'Children with great delight eat the berries thereof when they are ripe and make chains and other pretty geegaws of the fruit'.

The dog-rose is the birthday flower for 9 July, symbolizing pleasure and pain.

Stray blossoms appearing in the autumn were a sign of the plague and the superstitious believed that the flowers caused blindness if passed close to the eyes in June, and violent earache if they touched the ear. Children used the hairy seeds as an 'itching powder', placing them down the necks of unsuspecting friends.

EVENING PRIMROSE

A tuft of evening primroses,
O'er which the mind may hover till it dozes;
O'er which it well might take a pleasant
sleep,
But that 'tis ever startled by a leap
Of buds unto ripe flowers.
John Keats 'A Posy'

COMMON EVENING PRIMROSE (*Oenothera biennis*) *Oenothera* is of uncertain provenance, although some sources suggest it is from Greek *oinos*, 'wine', and *thera*, 'hunting or pursuing', and so imbibing, the root of one of the species being regarded by the Romans as an incentive to wine drinking much as one would have olives or nuts today. Others say that it dispelled the effects of wine. A very old name for the plant was *onagra*, ass food.

This native American plant was introduced from Virginia to Padua in 1619 and then to England about the same period. Evening primrose is not mentioned by earlier writers although the botanist John Goodyer in 1621 gave a detailed account of the flowers: 'the yealow cheives [stamens] growing from the nailes of the inner parts of the leaves, of the length of the pointell; which flowers are of a strong fulsome smell'. By the seventeenth century, herbalist and gardener John Parkinson (1567–1650), who was also an apothecary to James VI, lists it in his *Garden of Pleasant Flowers*, published in 1629 as the *Prime-rose Tree* or *Tree-Primrose of Virginia*.

This handsome flower is cultivated in various shades of yellow and even snow white and the delicately fragrant blooms are fertilized by twilight flying insects.

> *When once the sun sinks in the west,*
> *And dew drops pearl the evening's breast;*
> *Almost as pale as moonbeams are,*
> *Or its companionable star,*
> *The Evening Primrose opes anew*
> *Its dainty blossom to the dew.*

It is also known by the delightful name of evening star, to which the poet Thomas Hood alludes:

> *The Evening Primroses appear*
> *In galaxies of verdant stars.*

The name is derived from the fact that the petals emit phosphorescent light at night.

In the language of the flowers evening primrose signifies constancy.

The young roots of the plant can be boiled or pickled and eaten hot or cold, although the whole plant is edible. It was applied externally and used as a poultice and as an ointment to treat minor wounds or skin complaints, and used internally for coughs, colds and gastric problems. In more recent times the plant has received much attention from pharmaceutical companies and a whole range of oils and medications are now produced from the stately evening primrose.

FORGET-ME-NOT

And simple small forget me not
Eyd wi a pinshead yellow spot
I'th' middle of its tender blue
That gains from poets notice due.
John Clare *The Shepherd's Calendar*

FORGET-ME-NOT (*Myosotis scorpioides*) The generic name is from the Greek, *mys*, 'mouse', and *ous*, 'an ear', referring to the shape of the leaves. However *myosotis* was the ancient Greek name for the madwort, not the forget-me-not. The old name for this pretty flower was scorpion grass, probably on account of the way the stem curls at the end, resembling the tail of that arachnoid and as a consequence was said to be a good antidote for its sting on the 'like cures like' principle. All the species are known by that name. Another country name is mouse-ear.

A romantic but improbable legend is associated with the name of the flower which is recorded in Mill's *History of Chivalry*:

'Two lovers were loitering on the margin of a lake, one fine summer's evening, when the maiden espied some of the flowers of the Myosotis growing on the water, close to the bank of an island, at some distance from the shore. She expressed a desire to possess them, whereupon her knight, in the true spirit of chivalry, plunged into the water, and, swimming to the spot, cropped the wished-for plant; but his strength was unable to fulfil the object of his achievement, and feeling that he could not regain the shore, although very near it, he threw the flowers upon the bank, and casting a last affection look upon his lady-love, he cried, 'Forget-me-not,' and was buried in the waters.'

> *Where time or sorrow's page of gloom*
> *Has fixed its envious lot,*
> *Or swept the record from the tomb,*
> *It says, 'Forget-me-not'.*

Historically the flower is connected with the House of Plantagenet; when Henry of Lancaster, later Henry IV, was in exile he adopted the flower as his badge. For many centuries the flower was regarded throughout Europe as the emblem of eternal friendship or love. A flower bearing the name of 'Soveine vous de moy' was used in the fourteenth century for weaving into collars, and was worn by knights. Forget-me-not designs are still incorporated into rings and brooches, and for centuries have been used in decorative ecclesiastical work in wood and stone.

In the language of the flowers it symbolizes constancy, remembrance and true love. Charles D. Roberts expresses this in 'Forget-me-not': and means exactly what its name says:

> *Nor hath the blossom such strange power,*
> *Because it saith 'Forget-me-not'*
> *For some heart-holden, distant spot,*
> *Or silent tongue, or buried hour.*

FOXGLOVE

> *. . . when the foxglove, one by one,*
> *Upwards through every stage of the tall stem,*
> *Had shed beside the public way its bells,*
> *And stood of all dismantled, save the last*
> *Left at the tapering ladder's top.*
> William Wordsworth *The Prelude*

COMMON FOXGLOVE (*Digitalis purpurea*) The generic name of this handsome plant is from Latin *digitus*, 'finger', and is said to have been given it by the Bavarian physician Leonard Fuchs, in his Latin herbal published in 1542. *Purpurea* is perhaps not the right adjective to choose: although the flowers are often delightful shades of purple, many are a pure white, and others have a prettily mottled corolla with crimson spots on a pale cream background. Country names such as bloody finger, witch's finger, fairy cap, dog's lug, dead man's bells, butcher's finger and folks' glove all reflect the shape of the flower. In Celtic folklore it is associated with uncanny superstitions, and from its poisonous qualities has the name of dead men's thimbles. Most of the other names imply an association with elves and fairies who, as Hartley Coleridge says, 'sweetly nestle in the Foxglove bells'. The earliest known version of the name foxglove, foxesglofa, is in a plant list compiled in the reign of Edward III Etymologists say the name is from Anglo-Saxon *foxesglew*, or 'fox music', because of a resemblance to an early musical instrument, a ring of bells on an arched support called a tintinnabulum. The idea of the 'foxglove' is fancifully expressed by Abraham Cowley, bearing in mind that the Roman goddess of flowers and spring was assigned various plants for her personal use:

> *The Foxglove on fair Flora's hand is worn,*
> *Lest while she gathers flowers she meet a thorn.*

In the language of the flowers the foxglove symbolizes a wish, youth and insincerity, and is the birthday flower for 13 August.

A Shropshire witch is reputed to have discovered digitalis; however certain mystical precautions were necessary when gathering the leaves, which had to be picked with the left hand, from the the north side of a hedge. Nevertheless, in the distant past they were used as an external application for wounds and ulcers on the legs, although an early botanical writer advised:

> *The Foxglove leaves, with caution given,*
> *Another proof of favouring Heaven*
> *Will happily display;*
> *The rabid pulse it can abate,*
> *The hectic flush can moderate,*
> *And blest by Him whose will is fate,*
> *May give a lengthened day.*

The virtues of the plant as a heart stimulant and diuretic were revealed by a doctor and botanist in *An Account of the Foxglove and some of its Medical Uses* by William Withering, which was published in 1785. He used the leaves in the treatment of dropsy and was said to be the first man to notice its action in slowing down the movements of the heart. At first he used a decoction of the leaves, then an infusion and finally powdered leaves, which were gathered prior to the flowering period. His observations were soon confirmed by other authorities and when he died in 1799 a foxglove was carved on his memorial tablet.

FUMITORY

And fumitory too a name
That superstition holds to fame
Whose red and purple mottled flowers
Are cropt by maids in weeding hours
To boil and water milk and way (whey)
For washes on an holiday
To make their beauty fair and sleak
And scour the tan from summer's cheek.
John Clare *The Shepherd's Calendar*

COMMON FUMITORY (*Fumaria officinalis*) The generic name is from medieval Latin, *fumus terrae*, meaning 'smoke from the earth', and the common name from the same source via Middle English and the Old French *fumeterre*. How the plant acquired its name is not satisfactorily explained; however, the ancient name was fumiter and according to an eleventh-century manuscript:

Fumiter is an erbe, I say
Yt spryngyth in April et in May,
In feld, in town, in yard, et gate
Yer lond is fat and good in state,
Dun red is his flour
Ye erbe smek lik in colowur.

Prior suggests it acquired its name earth-smoke from the belief that it was produced without seed from vapours rising from the earth. Other writers, whilst agreeing on the derivation of the common and botanical names, suggest it may have arisen because from a distance the wispy greyish-green foliage looks like smoke. Pliny, on the other hand, says it took its name from causing the eyes to water when applied to them, as smoke does.

Country names of the fumitory generally reflect its meaning, such as vapour, earth-smoke, fumus, fumiterry, but also beggary and mother of thousands.

In the language of the flowers fumitory symbolizes spleen, and is the birthday flower for 1 September meaning 'Ill at ease'.

According to the ancient exorcists, when the plant is burned its smoke has the power to expel evil spirits, and it was used for this purpose in the famous geometrical garden of St Gall. The Victorian writer Anne Pratt, commenting on this now rare plant, wrote: 'One can hardly walk into a cornfield without finding a spray of fumitory . . . in summer the neglected cornfield is often quite red with the blossoms of this plant. This plant retains all its properties when dried. It has a very strong saline flavour, and it is particularly wholesome for cattle'. William Shakespeare was less complimentary in *King Lear*.

> *Crown'd with rank Fumiter and Furrow-weeds*
> *With Burdocks, Hemlock, Nettles, Cuckoo Flowers,*
> *Darnel, and all the idle weeds that grow*
> *In are sustaining Corn.*

Herbalists used the juice of the fumitory with dock and vinegar for cleansing sores and pimples and a distillation of the plant with honey and water was recommended as a soothing gargle.

GOLDEN ROD

Reaching up through bush and briar,
Sumptuous brow and heart of fire,
Flaunting high its wind-rocked plume,
Brave with wealth of native bloom, –
Golden rod!
Elaine Goodale Eastman 'Golden Rod'

GOLDEN ROD (*Solidago virgaurea*) The generic name is from Latin *solido*, 'to make whole or strengthen', on account of the supposed qualities in healing wounds. *Virgaurea* means 'rodlike'. The common name refers to the appearance of this attractive ornamental plant which is the only one of over eighty species native to Great Britain; most of the others were imported from America.

Country names for the golden rod generally reflect the shape of the plant or the colour of the flower, such as yellow rod, goldruthe, Aaron's rod, cast-the-spear, solidago and woundwort. It is also known as farewell-summer, which the nineteenth-century poet John Greenleaf Whittier alludes to in his poem 'The Last Walk in Autumn'; the tall stems, with their colourful sprays of blossom, have been replaced by numerous downy seeds:

Along the rivers' summer walk
The withered tufts of asters nod;
And trembles on its arid stalk
The hoar plume of the golden-rod.

Golden rod is the birthday flower for 30 November, and is symbolic of encouragement and precaution. Astrologically it is assigned to the planet Venus and is the flower of Virgo. Believers in the occult thought the plant could point the way to hidden springs of water and treasures of gold and silver.

Although it does not seem to have been mentioned by ancient writers, it was highly valued as a herb for healing wounds, both internal and external, and was imported for this reason alone in the Middle Ages. The popularity of the plant diminished somewhat when it was discovered growing wild in England. John Gerard, the herbalist, wryly observed: 'In my remembrance I have knowne the dry herbe which came from beyond the sea sold in Bucklersbury in London for halfe a crowne for a hundred-weight of it: which plainely setteth forth our inconstancie and sudden mutabilitie, esteemimg no longer of any thing, how pretious soever it be, than whilest it is strange and rare. This verifieth our English proverbe, Far fetcht and deare bought is best for Ladies.' Bucklersbury Street was where the Elizabethans held their herb-market.

A lotion extracted from the golden rod was used to treat ulcers, especially in the mouth and throat. Culpepper recommended the herb to fasten loose teeth and 'green or dry, or the distilled water thereof, is very effectual for inward bruises; as also to be outwardly applied it stayeth bleeding in any part of the body, and of wounds'. He also confirmed the plant's reputation as 'a sovereign wound herb, inferior to none both for inward and outward hurt; green wounds and old sores, are quickly cured therewith'. In more recent times golden rod has been used in the treatment of hay fever and tuberculosis, also urinary and kidney infections.

GORSE

Mountain blossoms, shining blossoms,
Do ye teach us to be glad
When no summer can be had,
Blooming in our inward bosoms?
Ye, whom God preserveth still,
Set as lights upon a hill.
E. B. Browning 'Lessons from the Gorse'

GORSE (*Ulex europaeus*) The generic name is probably from Celtic *uile-ex*, 'all prickles', most of the species being very spiny. Gorse is from Old English *gorst*, 'a waste', in reference to the shrub's natural habitat in the British Isles of commons and moor.

Although it gives the appearance of being sturdy it can be destroyed by sharp frosts; the Swedish botanist Linnaeus lamented that he could not keep it in Sweden, even in his greenhouse, and is alleged to have fallen on his knees when he first saw it growing in England, thanking God for such a beautiful flower. Elizabeth Barret Browning wrote of the occasion:

Mountain gorses, since Linnaeus
Knelt beside you on the sod,
For your beauty thanking God.

Gorse has several country names, such as furze, whin, prickly broom, ruffet and goss.

In the language of the flowers gorse is symbolic of anger, enduring affection and love for all seasons, and is the birthday flower for 28 November. Astrologically it is a plant of Mars. In the Druidic calendar it typifies the young sun at the spring equinox, when fires of gorse were lit on the hills; at Midsummer, blazing branches were used in the celebrations and were carried round the cattle to ensure good health in the coming year. Because gorse is said to be the first flower of the year to be visited by bees, it was believed to be enchanted and was consequently used as a charm against witches.

The golden yellow flower has a powerful scent which perfumes the air and although the blossoms open in early spring to autumn they can be found blooming practically all the year round, which is fortunate for an agreeable old custom, as there is a saying:

> *When Gorse is out of bloom,*
> *Kissing's out of season.*

For this reason, in some parts of the country, a sprig of gorse was inserted into the bridal bouquet.

However, a less fortunate association is that commemorating St Stephen's Day, 26 December, also known as Wrenning Day, when a wren was stoned to death in memory of the saint's martyrdom and carried round on this prickly shrub by boys begging for money. Allan Johnson's 'A Suffolk Calendar', refers to this barbaric ritual.

> *The wren, the wren, the king of the birds,*
> *Was caught St Stephen's Day in the furze*
> *Then pray kind gentlemen, give him (or us) a treat.*

As with several plants it was thought to be unlucky if brought into the home.

Gorse provides shelter for gamebirds and was used in earlier times for hedges and enclosures for cattle. Well-bruised shoots were used as a nutritious cattle fodder; cows were said to give good milk on this food alone and horses ate it with relish.

GROUND IVY

They spring, they bud, they blossom fresh and fair,
And deck the world with their rich pompous
shows;
Yet no man for them taketh pains or care,
Yet no man to them can his careful pains
compare.
Edmund Spenser 'Flowers'

GROUND IVY (*Glechoma hederacea*) Older writers claim the generic name originates from one given by Dioscorides, from Greek *glechon*, 'the mint pennyroyal'; the specific name means ivylike. Despite its common name there is no botanical connection with ivy and the name is attributed from the shape of the leaf; it is a member of the mint family.

Country names for the plant include Gill-go-by-the-hedge, hen and chickens, hedgemaids, Lizzy-run-up-the-hedge, cat's-foot, tun-hoof and alehoof. The whole plant has an aromatic, bitter taste due to the volatile oil contained in the glands on the under surface of the leaves. It was one of the principal plants used by the Saxons to clarify beer, the leaves being steeped in hot liquor which not only improved the flavour and keeping qualities of the beer but made it clearer, and many of the popular names reflect the plant's use in the brewing industry before the introduction of hops. The name gill is from the French *guiller*, 'to ferment beer', but as gill also meant 'a girl' in Middle English it was also called hedgemaids.

Because it was used to clarify ale it could be found in most cottage gardens, where it was also used as a cooling beverage which was known in the country as gill tea; the recipe consisted of 1 oz of the herb infused in a pint of boiling water, sweetened with honey or liquorice and drunk when cool; one wineglass three or four times a day was recommended for coughs, kidney complaints and consumption, and to purify the blood. The whole herb was gathered in early May when the flowers are still fresh and such was the demand for the plant that it was one of the 'cries' of London:

Here's fine Rosemary, Sage and Thyme.
Come, buy my Ground Ivy.

An infusion of the plant was also used as a wash for sore and weak eyes and John Gerard the herbalist further suggested that 'it is commended against the humming noise and ringing sound of the ears, being put into them, and for them that are hard of hearing'. Other writers included celandine and daisy with ground ivy, in equal quantities: 'stamped and strained and a little sugar and rosewater put thereto, and dropt into the eyes, [it] takes away all manner of inflammation, yea, although the sight were well-nigh gone. It is proved to be the best medicine in the world.'

The expressed juice from the plant 'may be advantageously used for bruises and black eyes' and combined with yarrow or chamomile flowers it was said to make an excellent poultice for abscesses and tumours. The somewhat astringent juice was also snuffed up the nose and according to Mrs Grieve 'has been considered curative of headache when all other remedies have failed'; a milder pain was said to benefit from a snuff made from the dried, finely powdered leaves of the ground ivy.

HEDGE BINDWEED

Yet what frail thin-spun flowers
She casts into the air,
To breathe the sunshine and
To leave her fragrance there.
Walter de la Mare 'The Bindweed'

HEDGE BINDWEED (*Calystegia sepium*) The generic name is derived from Greek *kalyx*, 'calyx', and *stego*, 'to cover closely', the calyx of some of the bindweeds being enclosed in two bracts. *Sepium* is from the Latin *saepes*, 'hedge', referring to its place of growth.

The leaves of the plant are arrow-shaped and delicate in texture, and in spite of the beauty of the large flowers, which are conspicuous for their snowy whiteness, bindweed is regarded as a nuisance by farmers and gardeners. Unfortunately it has twining stems that creep and extend in tangles over other plants and hedges and the root system penetrates in a dense mass, exhausting the soil.

The bindweed roots pierce down
Deeper than men do lie
Laid in their dark-shut graves
Their slumbering kinsmen by

wrote Walter de la Mare. In the Middle Ages, it is no surprise to discover, it was known as the Devil's plant and became known as Devil's guts, a name also applied to the dodder, *Cuscuta epithymum*. Country names include hedge convolvulus, hooded bindweed, bear bind, Robin-run-in-the-hedge, harvest lily and old man's night cap.

The flowers bloom in England from July to September and like all the other species expand during the sunshine and remain closed during dull weather, which in former days at harvest-time was a useful weather oracle; children would also amuse themselves sporting in the fields with the large, flimsy white bells over their noses, breathing in to keep them there.

According to the Victorian writer Anne Pratt, while some twining plants follow the apparent course of the sun and turn round the supporting stem from left to right, the hedge bindweed twines contrary to the sun, from right to left, and never otherwise. If the gardener turns it in another direction and it is unable to disengage itself and assume its natural bias, it will eventually die. Norman Nicholson made a charming observation on one of the bindweed family:

> *Up tall*
> *Turrets of sorrel the bindweed climbs*
> *Like a spiral staircase.*

Hedge bindweed is the birthday flower for 12 April with the sentiment obstinacy and insinuation. The small bindweed signifies humility.

Herbalists recommended an expressed juice from the roots or freshly gathered ones boiled in ale as a 'powerful drastic purge' for those of a strong constitution – 'on account of the nausea which it tends to produce, it is not considered fit for the delicate'. The plant was also used in the treatment of dropsy and jaundice.

HELIOTROPE

Or the faint, fair heliotrope,
who hangs,
Like a bashful maid her head.
Phoebe Cary 'Spring Flowers'

HELIOTROPE (*Heliotropium arborescens*) The generic and common names are the Greek name for the flower, *heliotropion*, from two Greek words: *helios*, 'the sun', and *trope*, 'a turn, a turning round or about', as the flower is supposed to turn towards the sun, following its course throughout the day. For this reason heliotrope are also known as turnsoles.

There is a flower, whose modest eye
Is turned with looks of light and love,
Who breaths her softest, sweetest sigh,
Whene'er the sun is bright above.

The ancients recognized this characteristic of the plant and in mythology ascribed it to the death of Clytie, daughter of Orchamos, who pined away in hopeless love when rejected by the god of the sun – Helios:

A symbol of unhappy love
Sacred to the slighted Clytie.

For hundreds of years this was a popular fable and during the eighteenth century it became the subject of moral reflection; James Hervey, in his *Meditations and Contemplations*, wrote: 'Let us all be heliotropes (if I may use the expression) to the Sun of Righteousness'. The classic heliotrope is not very well known, although it has been said of its fragrance 'that the heliotrope bears to the flower garden the same relationship that soul does to beauty, or love to youth', and another country name, cherry pie, refers to this unusual fragrance, conjuring up a culinary delight.

During the Middle Ages, when flower dials were fashionable, particularly in monastery gardens, heliotrope marked one of the hours. Andrew Marvell (1621–78) wrote of this delightful custom in his poem 'The Garden':

> *How well the skilful gardener drew*
> *Of flowers and herbs this dial new,*
> *where from above the milder sun*
> *Does through a fragrant zodiac run;*
> *And, as it works, the industrious bee*
> *Computes its time as well as we.*
> *How could such sweet and wholesome hours*
> *Be reckoned but with herbs and flowers!*

HENBANE

On hills of dust the henbane's faded green,
And pencil'd flowers of sickly scent is seen.
At the wall's base the fiery nettle springs,
With fruit globose and fierce with poisoned stings.
George Crabbe 'The Borough'

HENBANE (*Hyoscyamus niger*) The generic name was given by
Dioscorides, long before the Christian era, and is derived from Greek *hys*
'a pig', and *kyamos,* 'a bean', because although poisonous to man, many
animals can eat the fruit without apparent harm; hence the country name
hogbean. Other names include Devils eye, Jupiter's bean, stinking Roger
and henbell, from the Anglo-Saxon, *henn-belle,* from the similarity of the
enlarged calyx of the flower to the scalloped-edged bells of the Middle
Ages; in old plant lists it is *symphoniaca,* which suggests 'a ring of bells to
be struck with a hammer'. Henbane means that it is harmful to poultry.

The sulphur-coloured flowers are exquisitely veined with dark purple;
unfortunately the lance-shaped leaves, which are deeply cut, release an
unpleasant smell when bruised. The spikes of capsules (which can be
skeletonized and bleached) are referred to by John Clare in his *Shepherd's
Calendar* (1827):

And hunting from the stackyard sod
The stinking hen banes belted pod
By youths vain fancys sweetly fed
Christning them his loaves of bread.

Astrologically henbane is under the sign of Saturn and in the language of
the flowers suggests imperfection. In mythology the dead in Hades were

crowned with it as they wandered hopelessly beside
the Styx, the principal river of the Underworld.

In ages long past the therapeutic effects of the
plant were well documented. It was used to allay pain
and induce sleep by the Romans, Greeks, Babylonians
and Egyptians, who were all aware of the good and the
dangerous qualities of the henbane. For centuries it has
been associated with witchcraft, causing convulsions and
hallucinations to those partaking of witches' potions. There are
many records of unfortunate people having suffered delirious attacks
and temporary madness from accidentally eating the roots.

Fumes from burning henbane were said to conjure up the
spirits of the dead and give one the power of clairvoyance. A trick
popular with tooth-drawers (dentists) at a time when people
believed that worms bred in the teeth was 'to burn henbane in a
chafing dish with coles, the partie holding his mouth over the fumes
thereof'. Small lute strings were put into the water to persuade the
patient that they had come out of their mouth.

If in your teeth you happen to be tormented
By means some little worms therein do brede . . .
Put henbane into this, and onyon seed
And with a tunnel to the tooth that's hollow
Convey the smoke thereof, and ease shall follow.

Because of the plant's narcotic properties it was used in medicine to
treat whooping cough, gout, asthma, bronchitis and rheumatism,
and was applied with vinegar to the forehead for headaches and as a
fomentation for swellings in the scrotum, breasts and joints.

HONEYSUCKLE

As Woodbine weds the plant within her reach,
Rough elm or smooth-grain'd ash, or glossy beech,
In spiral rings ascends the trunk and lays
Her golden tassels on the leafy sprays;
But does a mischief while she lends a grace,
Slackening its growth by such a strict embrace.
William Cowper 'The Garden'

HONEYSUCKLE (*Lonicera periclymenum*) The generic name was given by Linnaeus in honour of the sixteenth-century German physician Adam Lonicer, who wrote among other works *Naturalis Historiae Opus Novum*, which contains curious information about plants. *Periclymenum* means 'to twine around with tendrils'. This is the taller growing of the two European honeysuckles, which is often found bound tightly around trees – hence its alternative name, woodbine. It belongs to the family Caprifoliaceae: this particular one is the English wild honeysuckle; the herbage of the true honeysuckle is a favourite food of goats, hence another name, goats' leaf. The name honeysuckle was given to the flower in the erroneous belief that bees extracted honey, when in fact it is of no use to them; however, children do enjoy sucking the nectar from the elegant, creamy-coloured tubular-shaped flowers.

Honeysuckle is the birthday flower for 20 November and symbolizes bonds of love, constancy and domestic happiness. In the language of the flowers it means, 'I will not answer hastily'. Wild honeysuckle is the birthday flower for 21 April symbolizing inconstancy in love. Coral honeysuckle signifies fidelity and French honeysuckle, rustic beauty. Astrologically the plant is under the dominion of Mercury.

A pleached alley was formerly a popular feature of garden design. It consisted of a hedge of sweet briar on one side with different types of honeysuckle opposite; planted along the edges of the alley would be other fragrant plants such as roses, rosemary, thyme, lavender and violets.

William Shakespeare, in *Much Ado about Nothing*, refers to such a delightful shelter:

> *Bid her steal into the pleached bower*
> *Where honeysuckles, ripened by the sun*
> *Forbid the sun to enter.*

Such beauty is not without its superstition, and Scottish farmers used to hang up sprigs of the plant in their cowsheds to prevent the cattle being bewitched. Nevertheless the sweet scent of the honeysuckle endeared it to many poets. Chaucer wrote of the delightful custom of girls wearing wreaths of flowers:

> *Wore chaplets on hir hede*
> *Of fresh wodebind, be such never were*
> *To love untrue, in word, he thought, he ded.*

Our native honeysuckle does have poisonous berries; however the flowers, in the form of a syrup, have been used for diseases of the respiratory organs and in asthma, and a decoction of the leaves for diseases of the liver and spleen. One old writer suggested that 'an elegant water may be distilled from these flowers, which has been recommended for a nervous headache'. Culpepper must have the last word, commenting that if you chewed a leaf you would more likely end up with a sore mouth and throat than cure it!

HOP

The sun in the south or else southlie and west
Is joy to the Hop, as welcomed ghest
But wind in the north, or else northerly east,
To Hop is as ill as a fray in a feast.
Thomas Tusser *Five Hundreth Good*
Pointes of Husbandrie

COMMON HOP (*Humulus lupulus*) *Humus*, of which *humulus* is a derivative, is Latin for 'soil', in which the plant thrives.

> *Choose soil for the hop of the rottenest mould*
> *Well doonged and wrought, as a garden plot should.*

Lupulus is probably from *lupus*, 'wolf', because like the animal it lightly embraces the host plant before destroying it. The English name hop comes from the Middle Low German and Middle Dutch *hoppe*.

The first reference to the hop would seem to be in the works of Pliny, who wrote of the young shoots being eaten by the Romans as we would asparagus – small bundles of the young hops were sold in the markets. The cultivated hop is best known for its fruit, which has a number of glandular hairs that exude a chemical, known as 'bitters'. It was first introduced to England in the early sixteenth century, in the reign of Henry VIII, as the old saying suggests:

> *Hops, Reformation, bays and beer*
> *Came into England all in one year*

although two centuries earlier hops appear to have been used in the breweries of the Netherlands. Sources suggest the planting of hops was forbidden in England during the reign of Henry VI although fifty years later limited cultivation was introduced from Flanders. Henry VIII forbade brewers to put hops or sulphur into ale as petitioners pleaded against the use of the 'wicked weed that would spoil the taste of the drink and endanger the people'. Edward VI granted privileges to hop growers but despite this encouragement, by the reign of James I consumption still exceeded domestic supply.

Many superstitions and customs were associated with the harvesting of the hops and to prevent luck leaving the field visitors had to contribute 'foot money'. Traditionally a Queen of the Hops was crowned at the end of the season and the hop pickers, whenever possible, retained a contorted and twisted branch as a good-luck charm. A festive Harvest Supper ended their labours which included a ritual of plunging young couples into the hop bins. According to Christopher Smart, in 'The Hop-Garden' (1752),

> *The exulting band*
> *Of pickers, male and female, seize the fair*
> *Reluctant, and with boist'rous force and brute*
> *By cries unmoved, they bury her i' the bin*
> *Nor does the youth escape — him too they seize*
> *And in such posture place as best may serve*
> *To hide his charmer's blushes . . .*

Hop is the birthday flower for 7 April, symbolizing injustice, passion and pride. Astrologically it is under the dominion of Mars.

Herbalists used hops to treat many complaints such as diseases of the heart and bladder and recommended hop tea as a sedative. Pillows of the decorative fruiting heads are still very popular for insomnia.

YELLOW IRIS

Thou art the iris, fair among the fairest,
Who, armed with golden rod,
And winged with celestial azure, bearest
The message of some god.
Henry Wadsworth Longfellow 'Flower-de-Luce'

YELLOW IRIS (*Iris pseudacorus*) The generic name is that of the Greek goddess of the rainbow, reflecting the variety of hues in the flowers of this family. *Pseudacorus* means 'false acorus' in Latin, so named to distinguish it from *Acorus calamus*, sweet flag, with which it was often confused.

In Greek mythology, Iris, daughter of Thaumus and Electra, was a messenger of the gods and is depicted in art as a beautiful young woman in a varicoloured robe with the wings of a butterfly carrying a herald's staff.

This distinctive flower is common along water margins and moist shady places as Shelley recalled in his poem 'Wild Flowers':

And nearer to the river's trembling edge
There grew broadflag flowers.

Yellow flag is one of many country names which also include such unlikely ones as skeggs, fliggers, livers and shalders, Jacob's sword, cegg and dragon flower, many of which liken the shape of the leaf to a small sword. Another old name, cucumber, refers to the seed vessel.

The iris is the birthday flower for 6 September and is symbolic of royalty, power, light, hope, eloquence and primeval power. In the language of the flowers it means, 'I have a message for you' or 'My compliments'. The petals signify valour, wisdom and faith. Iris is the flower governing the zodiac sign of Gemini.

In ancient times the iris was a symbol of conquerors and it is said that in ancient Eygpt, when King Thutmosis III returned home victorious from battles in Syria, making Eygpt the master of the empire, he held aloft an iris which became the symbol of his country where it was carved on the temple walls, royal sceptres and the brow of the Sphinx.

This and other species of iris have been referred to as fleur-de-lis or fleur-de-luce and according to legend, during the sixth century the army of King Clovis of France escaped defeat at the hands of the Goths by fording the River Rhine where they noticed the yellow flag growing towards the centre – indicating shallow water. Having prayed for victory to the god of his Christian wife, Clothilde, he adopted her faith and in gratitude, changed his emblem of three toads on his banner to three iris flowers, the iris being dedicated to the Virgin Mary. It is also known as the lily of France – this is because both irises and daffodils were often referred to as lilies in earlier times. In the twelfth century Louis VII of France adopted the flower as the emblem on his shield during the Crusades.

The iris was formerly held in high esteem by herbalists, who used the juice of the root for coughs, convulsions and dropsy. A plaster of the root, mixed with rosewater, was said to remove bruises and the sweet, powdered root sprinkled among linen and clothes found favour as a moth repellent.

IVY

The stateliest building man can raise,
Is the ivy's food at last.
Creeping on where time has been,
A rare old plant is the ivy green.
Charles Dickens 'The Ivy Green'

COMMON IVY (*Hedera helix*) The generic name is the ancient Latin name for the plant. Country names for this well-known evergreen climber with dark green glossy leaves are love stone and bindwood.

Ivy is the birthday flower for 13 March, symbolizing a need for support, obscurity, fidelity, immortality, tenacity, ambition and wedded love. In the language of the flowers it means, 'I die where I cling'. A sprig of ivy is the birthday flower for 24 September, symbolic of longing, and in the language of the flowers it signifies, 'I desire to please'. Ivy is a burial flower because it symbolizes immortality and an evil omen because it kills whatever it embraces. However its spiral growth is dedicated to the Resurrection, and the plant itself is a Christian symbol of attachment, death and undying affection. In Greek antiquity the ivy wreath is the emblem of Thalia, muse of comedy. It is dedicated to Dionysus and was thought to prevent drunkenness; his priestesses carried staves entwined with the plant during their sacrificial rites. Because of the plant's pagan associations the custom of decorating churches and houses at Christmas was at one time banned by early Councils of the Church.

Nevertheless, Felicia Hemans (1793–1835) offered her tribute of praise to the ivy and its glorious past in one of her poems:

The Roman, on his battle plains,
Where kings before his eagles bent,

Entwined thee with exulting strains
Around the victor's tent.

Superstitious people looked to the ivy as
a means of divination. One particular
ceremony took place on New Year's Eve,
when an ivy leaf was placed in a bowl of
water and left, untouched, until Twelfth
Night. If the leaf remained fresh a happy
year would follow; black spots
appearing near the apex of the leaf warned of leg and foot
complaints; spots in or near the centre suggested a stomach disorder;
and markings towards the stem were a sign of head and neck
problems. General decay of the leaf, unfortunately, signified an early
death. Ivy growing on the walls of a house was believed to protect
the occupants against witchcraft – however if the plant died ill
fortune was inevitable. In Wales it meant that the house would pass
into other hands either through lack of heirs or financial problems.

Many plants were used as love oracles, and in the case of the
ivy a girl would place a leaf in her pocket and go for a walk and the
first man she met would eventually become her husband.

Pliny observed in *The History of the World* (*c.* AD 77), that the
yellow berries were a good remedy against jaundice and prevented
drunkenness. The mythological background of the plant perpetuated
its association with intoxicating drinks: in fact a bunch of ivy on a
long pole anchored in a hedge was one of the first inn signs. This
custom gave rise to the saying 'a good wine needs no bush',
suggesting that the reputation should be good enough without
further comment. Water and wine mixed together in a bowl carved
from ivy wood were said to separate automatically, which led people
to believe in a strange way that the leaves and berries were an
excellent remedy after an excess of alcohol.

LAVENDER

Now summer goes –
Lingers, bestows
One rich last gift of her making –
These azure-dim,
Odorous, slim,
Lavender blooms for our taking.
Agnes Falconer 'Lavender'

ENGLISH LAVENDER (*Lavandula angustifolia*). The generic name is indirectly from the Latin *lavare*, 'to wash', via the medieval Latin name for lavender, *lavandula*; for many centuries the plant has been used as an oil to scent bath water and more recently soap. The Greeks named it *nardos*, from Naarda in Syria, and it became known as *nard*. It is native to the Mediterranean region and although there are several species earlier writers made no distinction between them; however, as the Romans were particularly fond of lavender it would seem likely that they first established in England this fragrant plant which at one time was cultivated commercially on a large scale in the London area – Lavender Hill, Battersea, is a reminder of past trading. It is recorded that Henrietta Maria, wife of Charles I, had a white variety in her garden at Wimbledon. Culpepper eventually wrote of it that it was so well known 'being an inhabitant of almost every garden, that it needeth no description'. The pleasure of having this aromatic plant with attendant bees and colourful butterflies is expressed by Margaret Brownlow in 'My Herb Garden':

My garden will have tranquil Lavender

> *Blue-mauve and pink and musical with bees*
> *To edge my path.*

Lavender bags and faggots have been used for centuries to perfume linen and clothes and the flower inspired one of the most familiar cries of London:

> *Lavender, sweet blooming Lavender*
> *Six bunches a penny today.*
> *Lavender, sweet blooming Lavender,*
> *Ladies, buy it while you may.*

As the oil of the lavender is largely volatile the spikes retain their fragrance longer if picked in the morning, as soon as the dew has evaporated. Nevertheless superstition warns that if the plant thrives in a garden the daughter of the house will remain unwed, from which came the saying: 'Lavender will grow in an old maid's garden'. This fact did not deter those who regarded it as a token of affection between lovers, as Michael Drayton wrote in his *Pastorals*:

> *He from his lasse him lavender hath sent,*
> *Showing her love and doth requit all crave.*

Lavender is the birthday flower for 9 January, signifying distrust, acknowledgement and assiduity, and is assigned to the planet Mercury.

Herbalists recommended two teaspoonfuls of the distilled water of the flowers to restore a lost voice and to 'calm the tremblings and passions of the heart', and the old ecclesiastical botanist William Turner promoted an unusual decorative idea when he wrote 'I judge that the flowers of Lavender quilted in a cap and worne are good for all diseases of the head that come from a cold cause and that they comfort the braine very well'. Small bags of lavender were often placed under a pillow to soothe a headache and induce sleep.

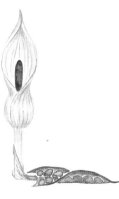

*L*ORDS AND *L*ADIES

The Lords-and-Ladies dressed for masquerade
In green silk domino discreetly hooded,
Hurry towards the nut-trees' colonnade,
Philandering where privacy's well wooded.
Victoria Sackville-West 'The Island'

L ORDS AND LADIES (*Arum maculatum*) The generic name is the Greek word for the plant. It is also known as cuckoo-pint and wild arum; the arum family, Araceae, has about one thousand members, mostly tropical, many of them marsh or water plants; this is our sole representative.

Oft under trees we nestled in a ring,
Culling our Lords and Ladies. O ye hours!
I never see the broad-leaved Arum spring,
Stained with spot of jet . . .

The flowering organs are contained in a sheathlike leaf, called a spathe, from which rises a fleshy purple clublike stem, the spadix, whose appearance has given rise to a number of indecent country names. The more acceptable ones include wake-robin, Devil's man and woman, bobbin and Joan, parson in the pulpit and stallions and mares; even Dioscorides suggested the herb was an aphrodisiac. The names calf's foot and cows and calves refer to the shape of the leaves, and Gethsemane is from an old Christian legend which tells of the distinctive markings on the leaf being caused by drops of blood falling from the crucified body of Jesus Christ:

Those deep unwrought marks
The villager will tell you
Are the flower's portion for atoning blood
On Calvary shed beneath the cross it grew.

Lords and Ladies is the birthday flower for 19 May, symbolizing zeal.

William Coles, in his book *Adam and Eve*, suggests a drastic means of deterring unwelcome advances: 'the fresh roots, cut small, will make excellent sport with a saucy sharking guest, and drive him away from overmuch boldness . . . for within a while after taking it, it will so burn and prick his mouth that he shall not be able to eat any more, or scarce speak for pain.'

The plant was used as a love charm by young men who wished to ensure they had the choice of the prettiest partner at a dance, by placing a piece of the herb in their shoe, saying:

> *I place you in my shoe*
> *Let all the young girls be drawn to you.*

During Elizabethan times a starch for stiffening linen was produced from the plant. Clear-starching was later regarded as an elegant feminine accomplishment in which gentlewomen liked to excel, but although the starch in the arum root was highly prized it irritated chapped hands so eventually the less glutinous root of the bluebell was prefered.

On Portland Island where the plant grew in abundance the dried roots were eaten by the poorer people and the powder or flour which was extracted was sold by London chemists under the name of Portland Sago as a substitute flour in times of famine.

Herbalists used the cool dark-green arrow-shaped leaves to treat skin complaints and draw poison from wounds and ulcers, and the juice from the leaves for 'stinking sores in the nose' according to Culpepper. A mixture of the powdered root and sugar was prescribed for coughs, and the berries soaked in brandy were given for loss of appetite.

In early autumn clusters of bright scarlet berries appear, remaining long after the leaves have died away; they are dangerous to eat, particularly for children.

LOVE-LIES-BLEEDING

You call it, 'Love-Lies-Bleeding,' – so you may,
Though the red Flower, not prostrate, only droops,
As we have seen it here from day to day,
From month to month, life pasing not away.
'William Wordsworth 'Love-Lies-Bleeding'

LOVE-LIES-BLEEDING (*Amaranthus caudatus*) The generic name is from Greek *amarantos*, unfading – referring to the qualities of some of the flowers. *Caudatus* means 'tailed', in Latin, from the shape of the pendant inflorescence. Amaranth was the name given by Pliny to some real or imaginary fadeless flower which among the ancients was a symbol of immortality, because its flowers retain to the last much of their deep crimson colour; this was much later likened, somewhat imaginatively, to streams of blood. The Greeks also used it when they wished to illustrate their belief in the immortality of the soul. The name is often applied by poets to some unfading flower which could be revived, much used by the ancients for winter chaplets. John Milton in *Paradise Lost* adopted the flower to crown the angels that bowed down before the throne of the Most High:

To the ground
With solemn adoration down they cast
Their crowns inwove with Amaranth and gold,
Immortal Amaranth, a flower which once
In Paradise, fast by the tree of life,
Began to bloom.

Shelley also mentions the flower in 'Rosalind and Helen', and its use in garlands, which were so popular with the ancient Greeks:

> *Whose sad inhabitants each year would come,*
> *With willing steps climbing the great height,*
> *And hang locks of hair, and garlands bound*
> *With amaranth flowers, which, in the clime's despite,*
> *Filled the frore air with unaccustom'd light,*
> *Such flowers as in the wintry memory bloom*
> *Of one friend left, adorned that frozen tomb.*

Love-lies-bleeding is the birthday flower for 31 March and symbolizes desertion. In the language of the flowers it means, 'Hopeless but not heartless'.

In spite of the earlier confusion surrounding the origin of the plant two or three ornamental members of the family have been grown in English gardens since Tudor times, although this particular flower was known to the botanical writers Gerard and Parkinson as the great purple flower-gentle. Under the now familiar name it appeared for the first time in John Rea's *Flora, Ceres and Pomona* of 1665 as 'an old flower, and common, called by some Country women, Love lies a bleeding'. The name prince's feather is usually applied to a similar species, *A hypochondriachus*, which has upright instead of drooping flowers, and it is possible that this is the flower that A. C. Swinburne referred to in his poem 'Love-Lies-Bleeding':

> *Stately shine his purple plumes, exceeding*
> *Pride of princes; nor shall maid or lover*
> *Find on earth a fairer sign worth heeding.*

MARIGOLD

Open afresh your round of starry folds,
Ye ardent marigolds
Dry up the moisture from your golden lids,
For great Apollo bids
That in these days your praises should be sung.
John Keats 'Marigolds'

COMMON MARIGOLD (*Calendula officinalis*) The generic name is from Latin *kalendae*, 'the first day of each month', because the flower is said to bloom, somewhere, every month of the year. Country names include gold ruddles, jackanapes-on-horseback, summer's bride, golds and husband's dyall, which was a favourite name of Thomas Hyall, who, writing in 1577, reasoned that 'the same shewth to them both the morning and the evening tide'. William Shakespeare said 'the Marigold, that goes to bed wi'th' sun, and with him rises, weeping'. In a couplet, written by Charles I when he was imprisoned in Carisbrooke Castle, a further reference, on a less happy note, is made to the sun:

> *The Marigold observes the Sun*
> *More than my subjects me have done . . .*

Older writers claim that the flower is so called in honour of the Virgin Mary and the poet John Gay in his 'Pastoral' poses the question:

> *What flower is that which bears the Virgin's name,*
> *The richest metal added to the name?*

Marigold is the birthday flower for 15 January, symbolic of cruelty in love, grief and pain. Astrologically it is assigned to the sun and the zodiac sign of Leo. As a flower of the sun it was considered lucky when brought into the home. Almost all yellow flowers were thought to be protective, as they reflected sunlight. Formerly a decorative flower for the festivals of pagan gods, the marigold is now dedicated to Lady Day, 25 March. In heraldry it typifies devotion and piety.

Marigold was one of the ingredients for a love salve prepared for St Luke's Day, 18 October – he was regarded as a lucky saint for lovers. Anyone wishing to dream of their future spouse had to anoint their stomach, breasts and hips with the ointment and repeat the following rhyme three times before they went to sleep.

St Luke, St Luke, be kind to me,
In dreams let me my true love see.

Herbalists recommended the juice of the leaves mixed with vinegar to soothe swellings and the flowers, fresh or dried, in broths. They also used the petals in puddings, to colour cheese and candied in preserves, and a recipe for wine can be found in Carter's *Recipe Book* of 1737. According to Culpepper a poultice made of 'dry flowers in powder, hog's grease, turpentine and resin, applied to the breast, strengthens and succours the heart infinitely in fevers, whether pestilential or not'. Modern herbalists have a more gentle approach, recommending an infusion of marigold for indigestion, gall-bladder disorders and the complexion.

Today the petals are used as a tea and with the leaves add a colourful touch to salads and omelettes. Skin and cosmetic preparations are produced from this cheerful garden herb which also yields a yellow dye, obtained by boiling the flowers.

MARSH MARIGOLD

May time is to the meadows coming in
And cowslaps peeps have gotten eer so big
And water blabs and all their golden kin
Crowd round the shallows by the striding brig.
John Clare 'Sport in the Meadows'

MARSH MARIGOLD (*Caltha palustris*) The generic name is Latin for 'marigold'; *palustris* means 'marsh growing' in Latin, the natural habitat of the plant.

This much valued rare ornament of the water margins has numerous country names which vary throughout the counties including water blabs, Marybuds, water dragon, horse blobs, May blobs and kingcups. Sacheverell Sitwell favoured the latter, as his poem 'Kingcups' indicates:

Great kingcups to that waste she threw
where nothing lived, and nothing grew;
Now, where poetry passed, there stays
The light of suns, the fire of days.

The English name marigold (it is unrelated to the garden variety) refers to its use during the Middle Ages as one of the flowers dedicated to the Virgin Mary – Mary's gold. It was also used during the May Day festivals, strewn by the superstitious across cottage doorways, hung in bunches upside-down in their houses and woven into the many garlands

decorating homes and churches. May was
the flower month, Flora's month, and the
Virgin Mary's too, and consequently
honour was paid to them with flowers
bearing their name and a Queen of the
May was chosen:

And the wild marsh-marigold shines like
fire in swamps and hollows grey
And I'm to be Queen o' the May.

wrote Alfred, Lord Tennyson in a poem of that name. The Floralia,
the festivals in honour of Flora, Roman goddess of flowers, were
formerly held from 28 April to 3 May celebrating the joy and
pleasure at the reappearance of spring, which gradually through the
centuries became May Day.

Let one great day,
To celebrate sports, and floral play
Be set aside.

Nevertheless there was a superstition associated with the marsh
marigold that it was unlucky to bring it into the home prior to the
celebration.

Herbalists used an infusion of the flowers for various kinds of
fits in adults and children and a tincture made from the whole
plant, when in flower, was given in cases of anaemia, in small and
well-diluted doses, as the plant was said to be 'strongly irritant'.

The buds have occasionally been used as capers by soaking
them in vinegar in the hope that the acid and poisonous content be
removed. The bright green heart-shaped leaves can be cooked and
eaten like spinach.

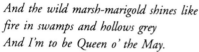

ℳEADOW SAFFRON

The Meadow Saffron magically sprung
By dawn in morning orchards in the grass
Near paths where shepherds on their errand pa
But ender-night beheld no crocus-colour there.
These in the sodden season unaware
That in their fragile temper they belong
Rightly to Spring.

Victoria Sackville-West 'The Garden'

MEADOW SAFFRON (*Colchicum autumnale*) The generic name is derived from Colchis, a place in Greek mythology famous for medicinal herbs where the flower is supposed to have sprung up from the spilt drops of the liquid given by Medea, prophetess, sorceress and later a dawn goddess to restore the lost youth of Aeson, father of Jason of the Golden Fleece.

This plant, whose flowers are usually of a lilac colour, is sometimes confused with the saffron crocus, crocus sativus, which also flowers in the autumn and whose stigmas yield the orange flavour and colour, but meadow saffron, which is also known as autumn crocus, is a type of lily, whereas the springtime crocus is an iris. Nevertheless, finding the flowers by chance in the autumn always takes one by suprise. Country names of this unusual native flower reflect generally its rather stark appearance – naked boys, naked ladies, naked nannies, star-naked boys and upstart. Victoria Sackville-West recalls two of the names which must have been in use near her home, Sissinghurst Castle:

> *those pure chalices that Kentish men*
> *Called Naked boys, but a lovelier name*
> *Others called Naked Ladies, slender, bare*
> *Dressed only in amethystine flame.*

Meadow saffron is the birthday flower for 3 April. In the language of the flowers it means, 'My best days are past'.

The root of this poisonous plant, which is a corm, and the seeds were used in medicine. Its highly toxic alkaloid colchicine was used to treat the pain and inflammation which occurs in 'gouty arthritis'; misuse, however, could severely damage the nervous system. This widely used remedy for gout was mixed with the powder from unburied skulls and prescribed for King James I by his physician Sir Theodore Mayerne. Old herbalists knew of the dangerous and medicinal qualities of the plant too, John Gerard warning that 'those who have eaten of the common meadow Saffron must drinke the milke of a cow, or els death presently ensueth'.

Earlier, Dioscorides tells us 'being eaten it killeth by choking like to ye mushrumps', which was later noted by William Turner, the Father of British botany: 'It will strangell a man and kyll him in the space of one daye, even as some kinde of Todestolles do . . .' Horace, the Roman satirist and poet, was also familiar with the reputation of the plant:

> *Or tempered every baleful juice*
> *Which poisonous Colchian glebes produce.*

In ancient Greece Theophrastus, philosopher and friend of Plato and Aristotle, reported that it was eaten by slaves to make themselves ill when they had been 'provoked or offended'.

MIGNONETTE

Mignonette and pansy fair,
With your fragrance scent the air,
While my thoughts in fancy roam
To your dear romantic home.
James Ballantine *A Bouquet of Flowers*

MIGNONETTE (*Reseda odorata*) The generic name is derived from Latin *resedo*, 'I calm', from the supposed soothing effect of some plants of this genus. It is a native of Egypt, where it was one of the flowers used to decorate the couches in the tombs. The name mignonette is said not to have arrived with the plant, which was referred to as 'the Yellow-flowered Aegyptian Bastard Rocket with the most sweet-smelling flowers'. The poet William Cowper refered to it as Frenchman's darling, although in France they use the Latin name reseda.

The sashes fronted with a range
Of the fragrant weed,
The Frenchman's Darling.

The connection may be found in the tradition that a lover will have success and good fortune if they roll over three times in a bed of mignonette! Nevertheless it was a favourite windowbox flower and Henry Phillip, writing in 1829, commented that it was grown for this purpose and that in London whole streets were almost 'oppressive with the odour'. Which in his opinion was no disadvantage 'where offensive odours are but too frequently met with'.

Napoleon Bonaparte is said to have collected seeds during his Egyptian campaign and sent them to Empress Josephine to plant in her new garden at Malmaison, and it was she who set the fashion of growing it as an indoor pot-plant for its perfume.

Mignonette is the birthday flower for 30 January, symbolic of health. In the language of the flowers it means 'You are better than handsome' and 'Your qualities surpass your charms'.

A romantic story tells how the flower became incorporated into the armorial bearings of an illustrious family in Saxony. The count was the intended spouse of the beautiful Amelia, who delighted in making him jealous. With her companion and cousin, Charlotte, a young lady with few personal charms, she attended a party where the guests were invited to select a flower. Amelia chose a rose and Charlotte a sprig of mignonette. As the flirtatious cousin danced with a dashing colonel, celebrated more for his conquests in the drawing-room than in the field of battle, Charlotte tried to divert the count's attention by asking him to write a verse for the rose. Seeing this affectionate trait in Charlotte's conduct he wrote:

Its life is granted for a day,
Its pleasures but a moment stay.

He then presented the cousin with this line on the mignonette:

Its qualities surpass its charms.

Amelia's pride was hurt and she retaliated by neglecting the count and by further behaviour which caused her ruin. He transferred his affections from beauty to amiability, rejoicing in the exchange, and to commemorate the event that brought about his happiness added a branch of mignonette to the ancient arms with the motto: 'Your qualities surpass your charms'.

Since ancient times herbalists have used the plant to reduce swellings and inflammation although the superstitious added a rhyme repeated three times, spitting on the ground each time.

MISTLETOE

The damsel donned her kirtle sheen
The hall was decked with holly green
Forth to the woods did merry men go
To gather in the mistletoe.
Sir Walter Scott *Marmion*

MISTLETOE (*Viscum album*) The generic name is the Latin word for the plant; **album** is 'white'. The common name mistletoe is from Old English misteltān, from *mistl*, 'different', and *tān*, 'twig', because this plant is so unlike the tree on which it grows. Host trees include apple, oak and hawthorn. Mistletoe is also known as mislin-bush, churchman's greetings and kiss and go.

Astrologically mistletoe is under the dominion of the sun. It is the birthday flower for 6 February, symbolic of difficulties. In the language of the flowers it means, 'You are a parasite', and 'I surmount all obstacles'.

In Scandinavian legend, Balder, god of light and son of Odin and Frigg, is said to have been slain with an arrow fashioned from mistletoe, the only thing in the created world that had not sworn never to harm him. This myth became part of the rites of the ancient Druids, who venerated the plant and the tree on which it grew, the oak: it is suggested that the name Druid simply means 'oak men'. Traditionally this parasitic plant was cut with a golden sickle and used during sacrificial rites. A white cloth was held under the tree to prevent the mystical sprays touching the ground as part of their belief that whatever grew on the oak was sent from heaven:

The fearless British priests, under the aged oak,
Taking a milk-white bull, unstained with the yoke,
And with an axe of gold, from that Jove-sacred
*   tree*
The Mistletoe cut down.

The Druids believed that the distinctive berries
were the fertilizing dew of the supreme deity.
After the ceremony the branches were distributed amongst the worshippers to be suspended
in their homes to ward off evil spirits.

In Greek mythology there is also a link of sexual significance
with the twin fruits of the mistletoe – Uranus, the personification of
heaven, was castrated by his son Cronus with a sickle and his
testicles fell into the sea changing into blood and foam, from which
rose Aphrodite (Venus) goddess of love.

The delightful practice of kissing under a mistletoe bough –
which was often decorated with ribbons, fruits and nuts – suggests a
strong belief in its phallic power. Custom, however, decreed that a
berry should be removed after each kiss and thrown over the left
shoulder. No berries – no kissing. In feudal times to cut and hang
mistletoe before Christmas Eve was to invite death into the family;
however, Hallowe'en was the exception. Before gathering small
sprigs of the plant, which could be worn round the neck as a witch
repellent, the gatherer walked three times round the tree completing
the ritual by cutting the mistletoe with a new dagger. According to
William Coles in *Adam in Eden* (1657), 'Some women have worn
mistletoe round their necks or arms, thinking it will help them
conceive'.

For centuries, herbalists have praised the virtues of the plant,
making use of the slightly astringent non-poisonous berries for
checking internal bleeding and 'falling sickness' (epilepsy).

MONKSHOOD

And London tufts of many a mottld hue
And pale pink pea and monkshood darkly blue.
John Clare *The Shepherd's Calendar*

GARDEN MONKSHOOD (*Aconitum napellus*) The generic name of
this poisonous garden plant is possibly derived from Greek, *akon*, 'a dart',
because it is said that it was used by barbarous races to poison their
arrows, although older writers suggest it is from Aconae, the supposed
place of its origin. *Napellus* signifies in Latin 'a little turnip', alluding to
the shape of the root. The Anglo-Saxons named it *thung*, which seems to
have applied to poisonous plants generally. It was then aconite, the
English form of its Greek and Latin name, and later wolf's bane, from
the idea that arrows were tipped with the juice or baits impregnated with
it to kill wolves; it was also used to poison wells and springs, usually as a
defensive action against invading armies. In former times it was also
known as the blue aconite and in Norse mythology Odin's helm, Thor's
hat or Tyr's helm, the shape of the purple flower suggesting the headgear
of the fighting gods. When the Benedictine monks settled in these
countries of northern Europe the cowl is said to have replaced the helm
of Tyr. By the Middle Ages it was firmly established as monk's hood or
helmet flower although this does not preclude such charming country
names as auld wife's hood, chariot and horses, captain over the garden,
luckie's mutch and granny's nightcap.

In legend the poisonous qualities of the plant were ascribed to the
foam that dropped from the mouth of the three-headed dog Cerberus
when Hercules, performing his twelfth labour, dragged the monster from
the nether regions – the flowers sprang up wherever a drop of spittle fell.

William Shakespeare in *Romeo and Juliet* compares
the effects of the poison to gunpowder:

> *Let me have*
> *A dram of poison – such soon-speeding gear*
> *As will disperse itself through all the veins,*
> *That the life-weary taker may fall dead,*
> *And that the trunk may be discharged of breath*
> *As violently as hasty powder fired*
> *Doth hurry from the fatal cannon's womb.*

It was a common belief that poisons were antidotes against other
poisons. Ben Jonson in *Sejanus* (1603) suggests the ultimate one:

> *I have heard that Aconite*
> *Being timely taken hath a healing might*
> *Against the scorpion's stroke.*

Although monkshood has been cultivated in gardens since before
1551 and is a favourite haunt of bumble-bees, writers down the
centuries have warned of the dangerous properties of this handsome
herbaceous plant, whose elegant flowering spire, set in leaves
distinctly cut into narrow-pointed segments, add height and strong
colour to any shady border: Henry Phillips warned 'that some
persons, only taking the effluvia of the herb by the nostrils, have
been seized with swooning fits, and have lost their sight for two or
three days'. Interestingly enough we are told that among the
common people the plant had the reputation for being the most
suitable for poisoning one's spouse – those of rank preferring
hemlock!

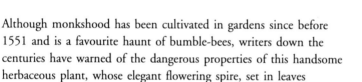

MULLEIN

Verbascums at twilight –
They glitter and glow,
Like lots of tall candle-sticks
Set in a row:
Like lots of tall candles
And glittering brass
They light up my garden
Whenever I pass.
Reginald Arkell 'Great Mullein'

GREAT MULLEIN (*Verbascum thapsus*) Older writers claim the generic name is from Latin *barba*, 'beard', from the shaggy leaves of some of the species. *Mullein* is said to be derived from Old French, *moleine*, from Latin *malandrium*, meaning 'the malanders' or leprosy. The name in its medical form, malandre, became applicable to cattle diseases, including lung problems, so the plant to remedy them became mullein or bullock's lungwort. Coles, in 1657 in *Adam in Eden*, says that 'Husbandmen of Kent do give it to their cattle against the cough of the lungs'.

Few British plants have so many country names, most of which refer to the useful nature of the attractive spirelike yellow flowering stem with its downy, grey-green decurrent leaves. The down on the leaves and stems makes an excellent tinder when dry, and the Romans named it *candelari*, from the custom of stripping off the leaves and flowers from the stalks and dipping them in tallow to make candles; it was known in England as candlewick for the same reason. As an old superstition existed suggesting that witches used this type of wick for their lamps and candles, another name was added – hag's taper; hag is said to be derived from haege, hedge, thus we find hedge taper.

The hag is astride
This night for to ride
The devil and she together.

In *The Niewe Herbal* (1578), Henry Lyte tells us that 'the whole toppe, with its pleasant yellow floures sheweth like to a wax candle, or taper cunningly wrought'. Our Lady's candle, high taper and torches were also in common usage. However, Jupiter's staff and Aaron's rod suggest the plant may have been used to ward off lightning.

Astrologically, mullein is under the dominion of Saturn. It is the birthday flower for 22 January, symbolic of nature. In the language of the flowers it means 'Take courage'.

The juice of the leaves and flowers was used to treat warts and the powdered dried flowers were taken to relieve colic. The residue from the fresh petals, steeped in olive oil and exposed to the sun, was an earache remedy, and a distillation of the flowers taken morning and evening was said to relieve gout. Twentieth-century remedies included the leaves dipped in hot vinegar and water and applied as a fomentation for tonsillitis and mumps, and an infusion of the leaves and flowers was prescribed for cough, colds and bronchitis.

NARCISSUS

All ablow,
White narcissi, pale as saints,
Save their eyes, where Nature paints,
With lavish brush, spring's yellow,
Mingle well with tulips mellow,
Or the lilies' lovely glow.
Constance Goodwin 'An April Morning'

NARCISSUS (*Narcissus*) The botanical name of the genus, and the common name, are said to be derived from Greek *narkao*, 'to grow numb', on account of the narcotic properties which the plant possesses. Popular sources, however, consider the derivation comes from Greek mythology and the youth Narcissus, son of Cephisus and Liriope, who spurned the love of the mountain nymph, Echo. Able only to echo the last syllable spoken to her, she died of a broken heart in a cave, her bones turned to stone and all that was left was the echo of her beautiful voice. The gods were angry and Aphrodite, goddess of love and beauty, punished Narcissus by causing him to fall in love with his own image which he saw reflected in a fountain; he died of languor being unable to embrace his love or avert his gaze. The gods, ever merciful, took pity on him and he was transformed into the flower that now bears his name, so that he could stand at the water margins gazing at his own image. Percy Bysshe Shelley wrote of the legend:

Narcissi, the fairest among them all,
Who gaze on their eyes in the streams' recess
Till they die of their own dear loveliness.

The cup in the centre of the flower is said to hold the tears of the ill-fated youth.

In Greek mythology the flower is dedicated to Hades, the god of the underworld, meaning death of a beautiful youth and decay that precedes new life. In Roman and Greek mythology the narcissus is associated with the Three Fates, sisters, Clotho, Lachesis and Atropos, who controlled the destiny of mortals, their birth, life and death; they were called cruel, because they did not regard the wishes of anyone. Originally they were worshiped as aspects of the new, full and old moon. The Three Fates wore wreaths of the flower in their tangled hair, the scent of which was said to be so painfully sweet as to cause madness, a stark reminder that narcissism, the symbol of egotism and conceit, will be punished in the end. Socrates, the great Greek philosopher, called the plant the 'Chaplet of the infernal Gods' because of its narcotic effects.

In the language of the flowers narcissus means, 'You love yourself too well'. It is the birthday flower for 28 January, symbolic of coldness, self-love, stupidity and one who gazes at his own image. It is the Christian symbol of divine love over sin, eternal life over death and sacrifice over selfishness.

The *tazetta* ('little cup') or bunched-flower narcissus is the one longest associated with man, even before Homer, who described it as 'wonderously glittering, a noble sight for all, whether immortal gods or mortal men'. Flowers of this species were used by the ancient Egyptians in their funeral wreaths, and have been found well preserved in their tombs.

NASTURTIUM

And gay nasturtium writhing up a fence
Splotching with mock sunlight sunless days
When latening summer brings the usual mist.
Victoria Sackville-West 'The Garden'

NASTURTIUM (*Tropaeolum majus*) The generic name is derived from Greek *tropaion*, 'trophy', the pillar set up in a battlefield by the Greeks and the Romans when celebrating a victory and on which captured armour and weapons of war were hung – the distinctive-shaped leaf was thought to resemble a shield and the unusual flower, a spear-pierced bloodstained golden helmet. Nasturtium is derived from Latin *nasus tortus*, 'distorted nose', in reference to the pungency of some of the varieties; the flower shape itself is similar to that of a nose. Because of its pungent taste it was originally named in error as the common watercress (*Nasturtium officinale*).

A species of nasturtium was introduced from Peru to Spain and subsequently distributed to France and Flanders. By 1597 John Gerard had received seeds from 'his loving friend John Robin of Paris', keeper of the King's garden. The plant quickly became popular.

John Parkinson referred to it as 'Yellow Larks Spurr, the prettiest flower of a score in a Garden'. Because of the spurred flowers, it was classified as a member of the delphinium family. By 1665, the plant was, according to John Rea, 'so well known that I need not be curious in describing it, for few gardens of any note are without it'.

Thirty years later Samuel Gilbert had further suggestions for the gardener and advised 'train these flowers on craggy poles and sticks a yard and a half high, to lead the wiery Branches which guided up by your hand to the top, make a glorious show'. John Gerard referred to it as the Indian cress, describing the form of the plant in a charming way: 'The flowers are dispersed through the whole plant, of colour yellow, with a crossed star overthwart the inside of a deeper orange colour, until the backpart of the same doth hang a taile or spurre'. The seeds were used as a substitute for capers. However, the flowers described by the seventeenth-century gardeners were not the nasturtiums we know today; the colourful scented and semi-double strains are of more recent times, easy to grow and welcome to visitors in any garden happily spilling out of urns, baskets and terracotta pots and climbing along fences and walls.

Nasturtium is the birthday flower for 1 November and symbolizes patriotism; a scarlet flower signifies splendour.

The fresh flowers and leaves can be eaten in salads and also add a decorative garnish to many dishes. Alice Coates amusingly observed that 'any caterpillar could tell you, the leaves contain up to ten times as much vitamin C as those of lettuce'. An old recipe entitled 'To Pickle Nerstusan Seeds and Flowers' advises one to 'gather the buds whilst they are greene, with the stalks an inch long' and John Evelyn recommended 'dry'd seeds of the Indian Nasturtium reduced to Powder finely bolted, from time to time made fresh, as indeed all other Mustard should be'. Herbalists believed that the plant would 'purge the brain and quicken the spirit'.

OPIUM POPPY

The poppy wears her silk and lace,
Clear-starched, with such delicate grace,
Her silken flounces hides and shows
As the wind goes and blows.
Katherine Tynan 'Poppy'

OPIUM POPPY (*Papaver somniferum*) The generic word is the Latin name for poppy and is said to come from the same root as the old Celtic word *pap*: *somniferum*, 'causing sleep'; Latin *opium*, from Greek *opion*, means 'opium' or 'poppy juice'. Because of the narcotic properties of some of the varieties it is associated with sleep and drug abuse – opium is produced from the sap of the green seed-heads. However, the edible seeds within the capsule do not contain opium but were used in bread-making and their oil for lamps, and were known to the Greeks and Egyptians several centuries BC. It is the oldest species in cultivation, and although its place of origin is unknown it was most probably introduced to England by the Romans and was certainly well known by 1597 as an ornamental garden flower. William Turner wrote of it as a medicinal plant, of which 'there bee many variable colours and of great beautie, although of an evil smell' added John Gerard; Elizabethan ladies named it 'John Silverpin, fair without and foul within'. Nevertheless by the eighteenth century many varieties and colours, some finely variegated, graced the country gardens. The plant was being used as early as the sixteenth century for its opium content but more surprisingly it was grown commercially at the beginning of the last century; patent drugs with innocuous-sounding names were readily available and such was the demand for opium that we became involved in a two-year war with China. Fortunately the invention of the hypodermic syringe in 1851 did regulate what had been a dangerous and haphazard means of dosage.

William Shakespeare refers to its use in *Othello*:

> *Not Poppy nor Mandragora*
> *Nor all the drowsy syrups of the world*
> *Shall ever medicine thee to that sweet*
> *sleep*
> *Which thou ownedst yesterday.*

Also Michael Drayton, who similarly describes it with other fateful plants in *Nymphal*:

> *Here Henbane, Poppy, Hemlock here,*
> *Procuring deadly sleeping.*

In Greek mythology the poppy is associated with Hypnos, god of sleep, loved as a benefactor of mankind and a bringer of sleep, who is usually portrayed with eyes closed carrying a poppy. His son Morpheus (the word from which morphine is derived) is connected with dreams, often depicted as a winged youth, holding a bunch of poppies, scattering their seeds to the wind. Somnus, god of sleep in Roman mythology, is usually represented as a young man of pleasing appearance carrying a poppy and a horn from which he dispenses sleep; he is said to have created the plant for Ceres, goddess of the harvest, to help her sleep as she was neglecting the crops because she was so tired after searching for her daughter who had been abducted while walking in a field of poppies and taken to the underworld.

Astrologically the opium or white poppy is a flower of the moon and is the birthday flower for 10 May, symbolizing consolation.

PANSY

Yet marked I where the bolt of Cupid fell.
It fell upon a little Western flower—
Before milk-white; now, purple with love's wound—
And maidens call it Love-in-idleness.
William Shakespeare *A Midsummer Night's Dream*

WILD PANSY (*Viola tricolor*) The generic name is the Latin word for various sweet-scented flowers, and *tricolor* means 'three-coloured' in Latin. The common name, pansy, whose older form was 'pawnce', is derived from the French *penseé*. Edmund Spenser gives the flower a place in his 'Royal aray' for Elisa:

Strowe me the grounde with Daffadowndillies,
And Cowslips, and Kingcups, and loved Lillies,
The pretty Pawnce,
And the Cheviaunce.

The flowers vary a great deal in colour and size but are either purple, yellow or white, or a combination of all these shades in each bloom, 'freakt with jet' as John Milton wrote in *Lycidas*.

In legend the wild pansy was originally white but Cupid shot an arrow and the wound inflicted on the flower changed the colour.

This flower, as nature's poet sweetly sings,
Was once milk-white, and Heartease was its name
Till wanton Cupid poised its roseate wings,
A vestal's sacred bosom to inflame.

wrote Mrs Sheridan; heartsease was the name favoured by the Elizabethans, although Shakespeare in *A Midsummer Night's Dream* used the juice of the flower as a love charm, which placed on the eyelids would cause the sleeper on awakening to fall in love with the first person they saw; he refers to the legend, but uses the name love-in-idleness. Other country names are numerous, often amatory and charming, including such gems as three-faces-under-a-hood, butterfly flower, kiss-her-in-the-buttery, call-me-to-you, herb constancy and herb trinity, which was dedicated thus by older writers because it has in each flower three colours.

Pansy is the birthday flower for 4 February, symbolic of heartease, kind thoughts, meditation, remembrance, trinity and unity. In the language of the flowers: 'You occupy my thoughts'; 'Think of me'. The superstitious counted the lines on a pansy petal – which should not have been bought but picked or given – as a means of telling one's fortune:

> *Four lines your wish will come true.*
> *Five lines there is trouble ahead which you will overcome.*
> *Six lines that a suprise is coming to you.*
> *Seven lines you have a faithful sweetheart.*
> *Eight lines your sweetheart may be fickle.*
> *Nine lines you will go over the water to wed.*

If the centre line was the longest it was most important that your engagement was announced on Sunday thus ensuring a happy marriage. If the lines generally inclined towards the right, that too was a lucky omen. Nevertheless to pick a pansy with the dew on the petals would cause the death of a loved one.

PASSION FLOWER

Though fair as any gracing Beauty's bower,
Is link'd to Sorrow like a holy thing,
And takes its name from Suff'ring's fiercest hour –
Be this thy noblest fame, imperial Passion Flower!
Bernard Barton 'Invitation to Flowers'

PASSION-FLOWER (*Passiflora caerulea*) The generic name is from Latin *passionis*, 'passion', *flos*, 'flower', and *caerulea*, 'sky-blue'. The passion-flowers are so named from a supposed resemblance of the finely cut corona to the Crown of Thorns and of other parts of the flower to symbols of the Passion of Our Lord. Formerly it was known as Flos Passionis, the flower of the passion, which Linnaeus cleverly Latinized into *Passiflora*, as the name of the genus.

The name passion flower is said to be connected with the conquerors of South America, who were cruel but, according to the beliefs of the time, pious in thought and deed: they saw in the flower the emblems of the story of the Redemption:

The leaf symbolizing the spear.
Five anthers, the five wounds.
The tendrils, the cords or whips.
The column of the ovary, the pillar of the cross.
The stamens, the hammer.
The fleshy threads within the flowers, the Crown of Thorns.
The calyx, the glory of nimbus.
The white tint, purity.
The blue tint, Heaven.

The flower remains in bloom for three days, symbolizing the three years of the ministry. An older version of this legend reveals an alternative mystical symbolism suggesting that the five sepals and the five petals signify the apostles, discounting Peter who denied and Judas who betrayed Jesus:

> *The corona is the cloud of witness;*
> *The circles become rays of glory;*
> *Five stamens are the five sacraments of*
> *   the Roman Church.*

or

> *Five points of the Protestant doctrine.*
> *Three stigmas are the Three Persons of the Adorable Godhead.*

Passion-flower is the birthday flower for 23 June and symbolizes holy love, religious fervour and susceptibility.

> *If Superstition's baneful art*
> *First gave thy mystic name,*
> *Reason, I trust, would steel my heart*
> *Against its groundless claim.*

The first passion-flower introduced to this country was the *Passiflora incarnata*, a native of Virginia, America, and was described by John Parkinson in his *Paradisus Terrestris* (1629) as the 'Virginian climer' or 'Jesuites Maracoc'. It is a sweet-scented climber also known as passion vine, maypops and maracoc. It bears orange-coloured berries, about the size of a small apple; when dried it is shrivelled and greenish yellow. The yellow pulp is sweet and edible.

A drug obtained from the passion-flower is said to be a depressant and with bromides was used to treat epilepsy. Because of the narcotic properties of the passion-flower, diarrhoea, dysentery, neuralgia, sleeplessness and dysmenorrhoea were all said to benefit from its use.

PERIWINKLE

Through primrose tufts, in that green bower
The periwinkle trailed its wreaths;
And 'tis my faith that every flower
Enjoys the air it breathes.
William Wordsworth *Early Spring*

PERIWINKLE (*Vinca*) Vinca is derived from Latin *vincere*, 'to bind', alluding to the long, tough runners of this mostly evergreen plant which was used in earlier times to bind down the sods on graves; in parts of Europe it was known as Flower of Death. The Romans probably introduced the herb to Britain, as the flowers were entwined into the wreaths used on ceremonial occasions.

Country names for periwinkle, whose flowers vary in colour from shades of blue to white, are sorcerer's violet and Devil's eye: (from a supposed connection with witchcraft), and blue buttons.

The poet Geoffrey Chaucer (1343–1400) knew the plant as parvenke, the source of the modern name: and in Macer's early sixteenth-century *Herbal* it is described as follows:

Parwynke is an erbe grene of colour
In Tyme of May he beryth blo flour,
His stalkys ain [are] so feynt and feye
Yet never more growyth he hey [high].

It is also known as joy of the ground; the lesser and greater periwinkle have attractive shiny leaves and this vigorous growing plant does make an excellent ground cover.

Periwinkle is the birthday flower of 31 January, symbolizing tender recollections. The blue periwinkle is the birthday flower for 18 August, symbolizing early friendship, and the white flower signifies the pleasures of memory. Astrologically it is assigned to Venus.

The superstitious regarded the uprooting of the plant from a grave with some awe, as the occupant would appear to haunt them. Nevertheless it was used as a countercharm against evil spirits and as an ingredient for love philtres; one particularly unsavoury recipe consisted of the powdered leaves, houseleek and earthworms, chopped together and taken with meals by a man and woman, to 'cause love between them'.

The plant's early association with death was extended to suspected criminals and it is recorded that in 1306 Simon Fraser, a supporter of Sir William Wallace, was taken to London 'heavily ironed, and his legs tied under his horse's belly; and as he passed through the city a garland of Periwinkle in mockery was placed on his head'. This gesture was common place during the Middle Ages as convicted prisoners were lead to their death.

> *Crowned one with laurer, hye on his head.*
> *Other with pervink, made for the gibet.*

The binding nature of the plant led to its recommendation by herbalists as a specific for those 'vehemently tormented with the cramp', in which the stems were wrapped round the limbs, and an ointment prepared from bruised leaves and lard was reputed to sooth inflammatory skin complaints and piles. The plant, generally, was used to treat toothache, ulcerated throats, diabetes and leukaemia.

PINK

The pinks along my garden walks
Have all shot forth their summer stalks,
Thronging their buds 'mong tulips hot,
And blue forget-me-not.
Their dazzling snows forth-bursting soon
Will lade the idle breath of June.
Robert Bridges 'The pinks along my garden walks'

PINK (*Dianthus plumarius*) The generic name signifies Jupiter's flower or divine flower, implying that this was one of the flowers dedicated to the King of the Gods on account of its beauty. Gerard claims to have given the plant its specific name, *plumarius*, because of its cut or 'feathered' petals. The name pink is said to be a combination of a Dutch word and an English word meaning 'a small winking or twinkling eye'. The word pink (as in pinking shears) also describes a scalloped edge, another feature of the petals. Pink as a colour was unknown at the time of the flower's introduction – possibly from the time of the Cistercian monks – and flowers generally were described as pale red, rose, blush, flesh-coloured or light red.

In heraldry the pink typifies admiration. It is the birthday flower for 31 May, and symbolizes amiability, divine love, timidity, welcomeness and morning light. The various colours and species of other members of this sweet-scented family also have a special significance and some have a designated day in the year, such as the double red pink, which is the birthday flower for 2 June signifying ardent love, the single red pink, which is the birthday flower for 3 March meaning pure love, the yellow pink, 3 June, symbolizing disdain, a white pink, fascination and talent,

and the variegated one, which means refusal. The
China pink is the birthday flower for 20 September
symbolizing aversion, Indian pink the birthday flower
for 25 October and the mountain pink, which is
assigned to 14 June, signifies aspiration. In medieval
art, the pink symbolizes divine love and signified that
a lady was engaged to be married.

Formerly messages of love, and sometimes rejection,
were exchanged by means of the charming language of
the flowers and it is to this delightful means of
communication that Leigh Hunt refers in his poem:

> *This art of writing billet-doux*
> *In buds and odours and bright hues*
> *Of saying all one feels and thinks*
> *In clever daffodils and pinks,*
> *Uttering (as well as silence may)*
> *The sweetest words the sweetest way.*

The pink is a native of eastern Europe and was certainly well
established by 1573 as Thomas Tusser, author of *Five Hundreth
Good Pointes of Husbandrie*, mentions 'Pinkes of all sortes' and five
years later John Lyte describes the unusual names by which they
were known: '. . . called in English by divers names as Pynkes,
Soppes in Wine, Feathered Gillofers and Small Honesties'. Today
the fragrant clove-scented pink is still the ideal plant for edging the
garden paths in cottage and formal gardens.

POPPY

Summer set lip to earth's bosom bare,
And left the flushed print in a poppy there;
Like a yawn of fire from the grass it came,
And the fanning wind puffed it to flapping flame.
Francis Thompson 'The Poppy'

CORN POPPY (*Papaver rhoeas*) The generic name poppy is the Latin name for this flower; *rhoeas* is possibly from Greek, 'pomegranate', which the flower and fruit were supposed to resemble.

Country names for this attractive flower include corn rose, *floreas rhoeados*, headache, Grenadiers and the red rose of Ceres, which in legend refers to the old belief that a cornfield scattered with scarlet poppies was the creation of Ceres, Roman goddess of harvest who taught men to sow and reap, and who always planted the flowers as gifts for the gods so that they would not take her cereal.

Formerly the flowers were primarily associated with farming. They were collected in dry weather in large quantities by an organized band of children, whose small fingers could gently detach the fragile, fresh petals, which they placed in muslin bags suspended from the neck, leaving both their hands free for gathering. The bags were carefully packed in straw and despatched the same day to ensure they did not lose their bright colour. The petals were used in the manufacture of a syrup (used as a colouring agent), those with dark spot at the base producing a deeper colour.

The plant has a peculiar heavy odour of opium when fresh which strengthened the widely held belief in recent times that smelling a poppy would give one a headache (which explains that particular country name), and also blindness and earache. Once the plant is dry it is completely scentless. The superstitious would use the leaves to test the affections of a loved one; in folklore they are known as tell-tale leaves, for when they are crushed in the hand they make a crackling sound, from which a sweetheart can discern whether they are loved or not. Theocritus wrote of this unusual omen:

> *By a prophetic poppy leaf I found*
> *Your changed affection, for it gave no sound*
> *Though in my hand struck hollow as it lay,*
> *But quickly withered like your love away.*

Like the hawthorn, it was considered by the superstitious very unlucky to bring into the home, and yet a formal design of the poppy frequently appears in Christian architecture, often at the termination of a bench pew as it signifies heavenly sleep and where one assumes it is purely decorative.

'And from the craggy ledge the poppy hangs in sleep' wrote Alfred, Lord Tennyson in 'Choric Song'.

The red poppy is the birthday flower for 10 May, symbolizing consolation. The scarlet poppy means fantastic extravagance and the variegated one, flirtation. Astrologically the poppy is a flower of the moon.

Although the flowers are familiar in the art world particularly through the influence of the French impressionist painter, Claude Monet, they have since the Great War become a beautiful floral tribute to those who died in Flanders field, where they have been cultivated for many years.

PRIMROSE

Ask me why I send you here
This sweet Infanta of the yeere?
Ask me why I send to you
This Primrose, thus bepearl'd with dew?
Robert Herrick 'The Primrose'

PRIMROSE (*Primula vulgaris*) The generic name comes from the diminutive of Latin *primus*, 'first'. Primrose is said to be a corruption of the Old French *primerose*, 'first rose', which is the name of the flower in Middle English. Country names include Easter rose, Lenten rose, darling of April and golden stars.

In the language of the flowers primrose means, 'Believe me'. It is symbolic of inconstancy, early youth, innocence, lovers' doubts and fears and is the birthday flower for 7 May. The red primrose, which symbolizes neglected merit, is the birthday flower for 22 October.

The superstitious believed, as with some other flowers, that it was a magic key whereby treasure caves could be opened – but then the power was lost. Children ate the flower in the delightful expectancy of seeing fairies, whose existence was shrouded in mystery. Later the poet Mary Howitt, who despaired at children working in factories, begged people to:

Gather the Primroses
Make handfuls of the posies,
Give them to the little girls who are at work in mills.
. . . (More witching are they than the fays of old)
Come forth and gather them yourselves,
Learn of these gentle flowers whose worth is more than gold.

In some parts of the country it was unlucky to bring less than thirteen primroses into the house as the number would indicate the eggs each hen would hatch. A similar claim is made with geese. Belief in the plant's protection against witchcraft on May Day is found in the old custom of hanging the delicate yellow flowers in the cowsheds to prevent the cattle being 'overlooked'.

Lovers used the flower as a love oracle, as Robert Herrick wrote:

> *Aske me why this flower does show*
> *So yellow-green, and sickly too?*
> *Aske me why the stalk so weak,*
> *And bending, (yet it doth break?),*
> *I will answer, these discover*
> *What fainting hopes are in a lover.*

A primrose with six petals was of special significance:

> *The Primrose when with six-leaved gotten grace*
> *Maids as a true love in their bosom place.*

Herbalists used the whole plant to treat rheumatism, gout, insomnia and nervous hysteria. Nicholas Culpepper advised the juice from the roots 'being stufed up the nose, occasions violent sneezing'. An infusion of the flowers was considered an excellent remedy against nervous disorders and John Gerard recommended primrose tea drunk in the month of May as 'famous for curing the phrensie'. In the seventeenth and eighteenth centuries the flowers were candied and pickled and also made into wine and vinegar, which required a considerable quantity of flowers. In ancient cookery the flowers were the main ingredient in a pottage called primrose pottage.

ROSE

'Tis said the Rose is Love's own flower,
Its blush so bright, its thorns so many;
And winter on its bloom has power,
But has not on its sweetness any.
Thomas Love Peacock 'The Flower of Love'

R O S E (*Rosa*) *Rosa* and rose are derived from the Greek *rhodon*, 'rose' and ultimately perhaps from *rodon* 'red'; the rose of ancient times was a deep crimson colour. The birthplace of the cultivated rose was probably northern Persia although many of our garden species are also native to the Mediterranean, China, India and Japan. As the rose became well known throughout the world, poets, artists and writers each endowed it with their own legends, so much so that it has generated more interest than any other flower, eventually becoming the symbol of the Western world and the national flower of England, though it was not until the Wars of the Roses (1455–85) that it became the floral emblem. The protagonists adopted their own symbols, the Yorkists a white rose,

> *I love no colours, and without all colour*
> *Of base insinuating flattery*
> *I pluck this white rose with Plantagenet*

and the Lancastrians a red one:

> *Let him that is no coward nor no flatterer,*
> *But dare maintain the party of the truth,*
> *Pluck a red rose from off this thorn with me.*

Thus William Shakespeare in *Henry VI part 1* set the scene. A further historical connection is with the House of Stuart, when the Duke of York became James II in 1685. A white variety of cabbage or Provence rose is said to be in flower on 10 June, a day regarded by Jacobites with great interest:

> *The tenth of June I hold most dear,*
> *When sweet white roses do appear*
> *For the sake of James the rover.*

Romans of the later empire were lavish in their praise and use of roses, scattering them at the feasts of Flora and of Hymen, and wearing garlands on festive occasions to prevent drunkenness – to them the flower was a sign of pleasure, mirth and wine. Roses adorned the prows of their warships and were strewn in the paths of victors and beneath chariot wheels. Brides and bridegrooms were crowned with roses, likewise images of Bacchus, Venus and Cupid. In classical legend, Venus presented the rose to her son Cupid, who gave it to the god of silence, Harpocrates, in the hope that he would conceal the weaknesses of the gods. The rose became an emblem of silence and subsequently was carved on ceilings so that anything spoken *sub rosa* remained secret.

In the language of the flowers the rose symbolizes love, beauty, elegance, frailty, joy, life, pleasure, secrecy, silence, bliss, a star, sun, wine, wisdom and woman. Various roses are assigned to different days in the year, each with their own symbolism; however the red rose, which is the birthday flower for 13 October, specifically means admiration, blushing, death, desire, embarrassment, martyrdom, motherhood and shame. A red rosebud is the birthday flower for 7 July, meaning pure, inclined to love and 'You are young and beautiful'. A rosebud of any kind signifies hope, promise and youthful beauty and a rose in full bloom over two buds means secrecy. A full-blown rose stands for beauty and engagement, a rose leaf, 'You may hope' and a rose thorn, death and pain.

ROSEMARY

What flower is that which royal honour craves,
Adjoin the virgin,
And tis strewn on graves?
Old Saying

ROSEMARY (*Rosmarinus officinalis*) The generic name means 'dew of the sea', in Latin *ros-marinus*, because the shrub was supposed to thrive best within the sound of the waves. Ros-marinus is said to be 'useful in love-making' as both Venus, the love goddess, and Rosemary (sea-dew) were offspring of the sea; Rosemary is her nearest relative.

The sea his mother Venus came on;
And hence some reverend men approve
Of rosemary in making love.

Astrologically rosemary is under the dominion of the sun and the sign of Aries and is the birthday flower for 17 January. In the language of the flowers it symbolizes affectionate remembrance as Ophelia in William Shakespeare's *Hamlet* says: There's rosemary, that's for remembrance. Pray, love, remember.

In ancient times, a bridegroom would be presented with a bunch of rosemary bound with ribbon by the bridesmaid, a herb for married men 'boasting man's rule, it helpeth the brain, strengtheneth the memory and is very medicinal for the head'. Rosemary was always included in the bridal bouquet and after the ceremony one of the bridesmaids would plant a sprig of the herb in the garden of the bride's new home which would in due course be used by her daughter.

Naturally the herb was used as a love oracle. If a girl wished to dream of her future husband she would place a sprig of rosemary and a sixpence under her pillow, the most popular night being St Agnes' Eve, 20 January, when the patron saint of young virgins was asked for help in all matters of the heart. A pair of shoes, one holding a sprig of rosemary and the other thyme, previously sprinkled with water, were placed either side of the bed with the words:

> *St Agnes, that's to lovers kind,*
> *Come ease the troubles of my mind.*

A vision of the future husband would then appear. On Mid-summer Eve, a bowl of flour was placed under a rosemary bush during the night and in the morning the initials of her future husband would be inscribed in the flour. It is said:

> *Where rosemary flourishes*
> *Missus will be master.*

Nevertheless, sprigs of rosemary were carried at funerals, which may have its origins in the idea that the herb had preservative properties against 'pestilential distempers'. The sweet smell of the plant would alleviate the odour of the corpse and the mourners would then throw their 'offering of remembrance' into the grave as they filed past to pay their last respects.

Rosemary is a symbol of the Nativity of Christ, and the herb, along with other plants, was hung in early Christian churches as a sign of welcome to elves and fairies. Traditionally it crowned the wassail bowl – a spiced ale cup – and at Christmas the main course was ceremonially brought in to the accompaniment of the carol beginning:

> *The boar's head in hand bring I*
> *With garlands gay, and rosemary.*

The Romans believed the herb stimulated the memory, binding it round their heads when studying. Because of its carminative qualities, oil of rosemary, distilled from the flowering heads, was used for headaches and stomach upsets, and rosemary tea was prescribed for colds. Our ancestors believed that to drink from a spoon carved from rosemary wood prevented one being poisoned, and a comb from the wood was said to cure baldness. The superstitious, of which there were many, believed that to make a box of rosemary wood and sniff it would reveal the secret of eternal youth, a quest that has occupied man for centuries.

SAMPHIRE

And in naked scenes,
Where precipice and needling rocks
Break to the sea with slope and spire,
My gold's the lotus, goldilocks
And patines of the stout samphire
Above unresting blue and foam
That round their crags and castles roam.
Eden Phillpotts 'My Gold'

SEA SAMPHIRE (*Crithmum maritimum*) The generic name is from the Greek **krithmon** or **krethmon**, 'samphire', and perhaps ultimately *krithe*, 'barley', to which grain the fruit bears a similarity. Samphire is probably a corruption of the old French name; it was formerly spelt *sampere*, or *sampiere*, from Saint Pierre. It is also known as sea fennel, although crest marine was the original name that was cried by the vendors in the streets of London.

Gathering samphire was an extremely perilous occupation which only the adventurous would undertake; it was carried out around the coastline of the British Isles. William Shakespeare in *King Lear* refers to the hazardous task of collecting the plant:

How fearful
And dizzy 'tis to cast one's eyes so low!
The crows and choughs that wing the midway air
Show scarce so gross as beetles. Halfway down
Hangs one that gathers Samphire, dreadful trade!
Methinks he seems no bigger than his head.

The danger of the trade, when the demand for this pleasantly aromatic and succulent plant was at its height, is described in Smith's *History of Waterford*: 'It is terrible to see how people gather it, hanging by rope several fathoms from the top of the impending rocks, as it were in the air.' The plant, which also grows in the clefts of rock, on the beach and even in the salt-marshes, was eaten raw as a salad, boiled as a vegetable or pickled, and it was in reference to the latter that Culpepper wrote: 'If people would have sauce to their meat, they may make some for profit as well as for pleasure.' Nevertheless he deplored the fact that the eating of samphire had gone out of fashion as it was a safe herb that was not only pleasant to taste but helped the digestion. Earlier, in 1597, John Gerard wrote of it: 'The leaves kept in pickle and eaten in sallads with oile and vinegar is a pleasant sauce for meat, wholesome for the stoppings of the liver, milt and kidnies. It is the pleasantest sauce, most familiar and best agreeing with man's body.' Pickled samphire is eaten today; however, it is best picked in late spring and early summer when it is green and fresh. Alternatively it can be cooked as a vegetable with butter.

Astrologically samphire is a herb of Jupiter.

An old story shows how a little botanical knowledge can be useful in times of danger. Years ago a ship was wrecked on the Sussex coast and a group of survivors found themselves marooned on a very large rock. To their dismay the sea began to rise and they discussed their chances of swimming to the shore before they were all swept away. One of the ship's officers saw samphire growing nearby and knew then that they would be safe, because although the plant grows within reach of sea spray it will not grow where the sea can cover it.

SCABIOUS

Then soon gay summer brings his gaudy train,
His crimson poppies deck the corn-clad plain;
There scabious blue and purple knapweed rise,
And weld and yarrow show their various dyes.
John Scott 'Rural Scene'

DEVIL'S BIT SCABIOUS (*Succisa pratensis*) The generic name is derived from the Latin *succido*, 'I cut off from below'; *pratensis* means botanically 'found growing in meadows', from Latin *pratensis*, 'a meadow'. The common name is derived from Latin *scabere*, 'to scratch', for which skin irritations some of the species were said to be a remedy. The root when fully grown is about the thickness of a finger ending in an abrupt way suggesting it has been bitten off, which gave rise to the legend that the Devil found it in Paradise, but because he thought of the good it might do he bit off part of the root to destroy the plant, thinking it would die. This legend is well known, even in Europe where the plant has a similar name. An older writer, whilst confirming the story, commented: 'old fantastick charmers report that the divel did bite it for envie, because it is a herbe that hath so many good vertues and it is so beneficial to mankinde'.

Country names for the Devil's bit scabious include ofbit, premorse scabious, forebitten more and pincushions, as Victoria Sackville-West recalled in 'The Garden':

   . . . or scabious tall
   That country children call
   Pincushions, with their gift

Of accurate observance and their swift
Naming more vivid than the botanist.

Devil's bit scabious is the birthday flower for 8 August, symbolizing unfortunate love. The garden scabious is the birthday flower for 26 June and symbolizes widowhood; it was considered an appropriate flower for a widow to include in her bouquet when in mourning for a husband.

The superstitious believed that picking the Devil's bit scabious caused the Devil to appear at your bedside that same night.

Herbalists used the distilled water or juice of the plant to treat sores, wounds and scurf, and a cosmetic preparation consisting of the green part of the plant boiled in water and mixed with borax was recommended to treat pimples and freckles. The powdered root taken in a drink helped to promote sweating in feverish complaints and expel worms. The root was also made into an ointment for skin diseases, and boiled in wine and drunk as a very powerful preventative against the plague and other 'pestilential diseases, fevers, poisons and the bites of venomous creatures'.

The whole plant or root, bruised and applied to the skin, was alleged to remove any black or blue marks; and in ancient times draw out pieces of arrow heads, broken bone and foreign bodies embedded in the flesh. Devil's bit scabious is collected in September and dried, after which a useful tea is infused to treat coughs, fevers and internal inflammation.

SCARLET PIMPERNEL

And scarlet starry points of flowers
Pimpernel dreading nights and showers
Oft calld 'the shepherds weather glass'
That sleep till suns have dyd the grass
Then wakes and spreads its creeping bloom
Till clouds or threatning shadows come
Then close it shuts to sleep again.
John Clare *The Shepherd's Calendar*

SCARLET PIMPERNEL (*Anagallis arvensis*) The generic name is derived from Greek *anagelao*, signifying 'to laugh', because it was said to remove the depression following liver troubles; according to Pliny, taken inwardly it promoted mirth.

Many of the country names associated with the plant reflect its use as a weather oracle –

And boys that mark them shut too soon
Will call them 'John go bed at noon'.

Scarlet pimpernel is also known as shepherd's barometer, poor man's weather glass and shepherd's weather glass, adder's eyes and until the sixteenth century, bipinella.

This delicate flower is sensitive to the weather and no other common plant has attracted such lore. According to a well-known proverb:

No ear hath heard, no tongue can tell,
The virtues of the Pimpernel.

The following lines are from the *Botanical Looker-out*:

Come, tell me, thou coy little flower,
Converging thy petals again,
Who gave thee the magical power
Of shutting thy cup on the rain?

Scarlet pimpernel is the birthday flower for 19
August symbolizing assignation, change, child-
hood and faithfulness. The flower also typifies
one who functions in the dark, and astrologically is assigned to the sun.

It was revered as a 'gallant Solar herb, of cleansing attractive
quality, whereby it draweth forth thorns and splinters gotten into
the flesh'. As a cosmetic herb, the distilled water or juice of the
scarlet pimpernel was used to 'cleanse the skin of roughness,
deformity and discolourings'. Scarlet pimpernel boiled with hog's
lard was said to be an excellent remedy for encouraging hair growth.

This tiny plant had a good reputation as a witch repellent;
however, a precautionary charm with religious overtones had to be
repeated when it was gathered:

Herbe Pimpernell, I have thee found,
Growing upon Christ Jesus' ground:
The same gift the Lord Jesus gave unto thee,
When He shed His blood on the tree.
Arise up, Pimpernell, and goe with me,
And God blesse me,
And all that shall were thee.

If one says this 'twice a day for fifteen days in succession, fasting in
the morning, and in the evening with a full stomach, no one can
predict how much good will follow'.

SEA HOLLY

I came on that blue-headed plant
That lovers ate to waken love,
Eryngo; but I felt no want,
A lovesick swain, to eat thereof.
Andrew Young 'Eryngo'

SEA HOLLY (*Eryngium maritimum*) The generic name is a Latinization of *eryngion*, an ancient name of obscure meaning which may signify a thistle-like herb (as it does resemble members of that family) which was adopted by the Roman naturalist Pliny, from the Greek Dioscorides, who praised its virtues. However, Mrs Grieve, in *A Modern Herbal*, suggests 'that the genus has reference to its supposed efficacy in flatulent disorders coming from the Greek *eruggarein* ('to eructate'). Dioscorides recommended the roots for this purpose'. The common name aptly describes the prickly nature of this attractive sea-green plant with its bright blue flowers which is also known as sea holm, sea hulver, sea eryngium and eryngo or eryngoe.

> *Eryngo to the threat'ning storm,*
> *With dauntless pride uprears*
> *His azure crest and warrior form,*
> *And points his spears.*

For Shakespeare in *The Merry Wives of Windsor* it had a similar name:

> *Let the sky rain Potatoes; let it thunder to the tune of Green Sleeves, hail kissing-comfits, and snow Eringoes.*

Kissing-comfits were a breath-sweetening lozenge made from the candied root of the plant during the reign of Elizabeth I. Later, the candied root was eaten as a sweet, when the apothecary Robert Buxton introduced them into general use, bringing fame to the town of Colchester. It is recorded that when Queen Charlotte, George III's consort, visited the city she was presented with a box of the sweet-meat.

According to the famous Swedish botanist Linnaeus, 'the young flowering-shoots, when boiled and eaten like asparagus, are palatable and nourishing. The roots boiled or roasted, resemble chestnuts in taste' and are equally agreeable.

Although sea holly adds colour to sand dunes and coastal areas because ideally it requires a sandy, saline habitat, several species were successfully introduced to the garden. The Elizabethans and Jacobeans were particularly enthusiastic about this handsome decorative plant with its ornamental foliage. Whether this was due in part to a reputation it had acquired from Saxon times as an aphrodisiac is debatable; the herbalist Gerard declared that the roots 'if conditioned, or preserved with sugar, they are exceeding good to be given to old and aged people that are consumed and withered with age, and who want natural moisture' and that they could also be used 'to secure a straying lover'. Rapin, in his poem 'Of Gardens', describes how to ensure constancy in a lover:

> *Grecian Eryngoes now commence their fame,*
> *Which, worn by brides, will fix their husbands' flame,*
> *And check the conquests of a rival dame.*

The magic of the plant, according to the Greek philosopher Plutarch (c.46–c.120), is related in a curious statement: 'if one goat taketh it into her mouth, it causeth her first to stand still and afterwards the whole flock, until such time as the shepherd takes it from her'.

SNAPDRAGON

Soon will high Midsummer pomps come on,
Soon will the musk carnations break and swell,
Soon shall we have gold-dusted snapdragon,
Sweet-William with his homely cottage-smell.
Matthew Arnold 'Thyrsis'

SNAPDRAGON (*Antirrhinum majus*) The generic name is from two Greek words: *anti*, 'like', and *rhis*, 'nose or snout', alluding to the shape of the flower. The common name is easily understood by those enjoying the children's game of pinching the flowers between thumb and forefinger, causing them to open in imitation of the fabulous monster or watching a heavy-weight bumble-bee disappear inside. The flowers are perfect traps for smaller insects; once admitted there is no return, but having consumed the nectar they break free from their dungeon by gnawing a hole at the base of the tube. There are other country names with animal connections – lion's snap, rabbit's mouth, bulldogs, toad's mouth and dog's mouth.

Antirrhinum, more modest, takes the style
Of Lion's mouth, sometimes of Calf's-snout vile,
By us Snapdragon called, to make amends
But say what this chimera name intends?

wrote Abraham Cowley. The name calves' snout, from a fancied resemblance to the nose and mouth of a calf, actually refers to the shape of the seed pods, of which John Gerard was less complimentary, comparing them to 'old bones of a Sheep's head that hath long been in the water, or the flesh consumed cleane away'.

Snapdragon is the birthday flower for 28 June and in the language of the flowers symbolizes indiscretion, presumption and 'no'.

A native of southern Europe, the snapdragon has been a familiar plant in our gardens for centuries, and has become naturalized in many places. Lyte wrote of it in his *Niewe Herball* as 'not much unlike the floures of Todeflax, but much larger and without tayles, of a faint yellowish colour. After them comme long round huskes, the foremost part whereof are somewhat like to a Calfes Snowte or Moosell, wherein the seed is conteyned.' By 1757 John Hill could write: 'We treat here of a Plant, which, though not a native of our Country, bears the free Air perfectly well in it, and sows itself freely like a wild Weed. The gardener will smile to hear us speak of instructing him in the culture of a Plant, that will live on an old Wall, and propogate itself from year to year without his Care.'

'The snapdragon, which is much cultivated in gardens on account of its showy flowers, is, in many places, said to have a supernatural influence, and to possess the power of destroying charms' wrote Dyer in his *English Folklore*. Even Theophrastus (*c.*320 B C) is quoted by William Turner as saying, 'that some men have supposed that the use of thys herbe should helpe men to obtayne prayse and worship . . . the dreams of sorcerers . . .' In complete contrast, in his poem 'Snapdragon', D. H. Lawrence was romantic and playful:

And in her bosom couched in the confines of her gown
Like heavy birds at rest there, softly stirred
By her measured breaths: 'I like to see' said she,
'The snap-dragon put out his tongue at me.'

SNOWDROP

Nor will I then thy modest grace forget,
Chaste Snowdrop, venturous harbinger of Spring,
And pensive monitor of fleeting years!
William Wordsworth 'To A Snowdrop'

SNOWDROP (*Galanthus nivalis*) The generic name comes from Greek *gala*, 'milk' and *anthos*, 'a flower', alluding to its whiteness, and the specific name from Latin, *nivalis* meaning 'snowy'. Familiar though it is, many authorities do not consider it a native plant: it is often found growing wild on the sites of ancient monastries and the bulbs were probably brought over by Italian monks during the fifteenth century, as it had an excellent reputation as a wound herb. It would also be grown for the religious ceremony Candlemas Day, the Feast of the Purification, in February when the image of the Virgin Mary, to whom the plant is dedicated, was removed from the altar and snowdrops were strewn in its place. This Church festival reflects many of the country names associated with this delightful flower such as purification flower, Mary's tapers, fair maid of February, procession flower and Candlemas bells, also snow bells and snow piercers. Because it grew in churchyards it was known as a death flower, recalling the white mourning for children, and therefore considered dangerous to pick.

The snowdrop is the birthday flower for 20 January, symbolic of friendship in adversity, hope in sorrow, and purity. Alfred, Lord Tennyson, like other poets, was aware of the symbolism of the flower:

Make thou my spirit pure and clean,
As are the frosty skies,

Or the first snowdrop of the year
That in my bosom lies.

Religious connections do not preclude superstitions
and there are several associated with this seemingly
frail but hardy plant. Girls who intended marrying
during the coming year would not do so if they
picked the flower before St Valentine's Day; it was
considered unlucky to bring one snowdrop into the house because
of its supposed resemblance to a corpse in a shroud – a death
omen; and not so very long ago most country people kept their
own poultry and until all the hens' eggs had hatched snowdrops
remained outside the home – otherwise, no chickens. Welsh border
people would gather bunches of snowdrops to purify the house and
in many parts of England it was customary for the first snowdrops
of the year to be hung on family graves.

Yes, punctual to the time, thou'rt here again,
As still thou art: though frost or rain may vary.

A bowl of snowdrops brought into the house on Candlemas Day
was said to give the house 'the white purification'. It was the
custom on this day for girls to dress in white and walk in
procession to church, which explains the earlier name, 'procession
flower'.

According to legend, when Adam and Eve left the Garden of
Eden snow began to fall and an angel, wishing to comfort Eve,
assured them spring would soon follow, by transforming some of
the feathery snowflakes into the flower.

SOLOMON'S SEAL

'Thou wert not, Solomon, in all thy glory,
Arrayed,' the lilies cry, 'in robes like ours;
How vain your grandeur! ah! how transitory
Are human flowers!'
Horace Smith 'Hymn to the Flowers'

COMMON SOLOMON'S SEAL (Polygonatum multiflorum) The
generic name comes from Greek *poly*, 'many', *gonu*, 'knee or joint of
grasses', referring to the distinctive markings on the stem or root. The
specific name distinguishes this many-blossomed species from those with
one or two flowers. Considerable ambiguity surrounds the origin of the
common English name: one explanation is that the markings on the root,
when cut transversely, resemble Hebrew characters, which suggested that
Solomon 'who knew the diversities of plants and the virtues of their
roots', had set his seal upon them in testimony of the value to man as a
medicinal root. Dr Prior, in his *Popular Names of British Plants*, is quite
precise: 'it is from the flat round scars on the root-stock resembling what
is called a Solomon's seal, a name given by the Arabs to a six-pointed
star, formed by two equilateral triangles intersecting each other, and of
frequent occurrence in Oriental tales'. A third source suggests that as the
flower stems decay the main stalk becomes scarred and the marks
resemble seals; as the roots were believed to have medicinal properties
they were used to seal wounds. The last is that the white pendant
blossoms suggest a hanging bunch of seals, with possible reference to the

ones suspended from the capacious waistcoats of our distant ancestors. Regardless of all these explanations the graceful curving flower stems, with their delicate waxy flowers, are reminiscent of a tintinnabulum – an arch of bells.

> 'Neath cloistered boughs, each floral
>   bell that swingeth
> And toils its perfume on the passing air.

Old country names include ladder to heaven, David's harp, Solomon's heal, Lady's seal and St Mary's seal (*Sigillum Sanctae Mariae*), the name used by the herbalist John Gerard, who maintained it was given to the root 'partly because it bears marks something like the stamp of a seal, but still more because the virtue the root hath in sealing up green wounds, broken bones and such like, being stamp't and laid thereon'. Solomon's seal was a very popular medicinal plant, as he also recommended that whilst the root was 'fresh and greene and applied, taketh away in one night or two at the most, any bruise, blacke or blew spots gotten by fals or women's wilfulness in stumbling upon the hastie husband's fists'. A concoction of the root, taken in wine, was considered a suitable drink for those with broken bones, 'as it disposes the bones to knit'. This remedy was endorsed with a further suggestion: 'the roots must be stamped, some ale or wine put thereto and strained and given to drink . . . as well unto themselves as to their cattle'. A distillation of the whole plant was said to remove spots and freckles leaving the face fresh, fair and lovely. Culpepper added, 'it is the principal ingredient of most of the cosmetics and beauty washes advertised by perfumers at high prices'. The flowers and roots were used as snuff to induce sneezing, thereby relieving headaches, and as an aphrodisiac in love philtres and potions.

STRAWBERRY

God has given a kindlier power
To the favoured strawberry-flower.
Hither soon as spring is fled . . .
Lurking berries, ripe and red,
Then will hang on every stalk,
Each within its leafy bower;
And for that promise spare the flower!
William Wordsworth 'Foresight'

WILD STRAWBERRY (*Fragaria vesca*) The name is derived from Latin *fragrans*, 'fragrant' and *vesca*, 'edible'. One of the earliest references to the plant in English writings can be found in the Saxon medical plant list of the tenth century, the *Leechbook of Bald*. In 1265 the streowberie or straberie, later known as strayberry, from the habit of the long suckers and their ability to cover the ground, is mentioned in the household accounts of the Countess of Leicester and in two different manuscripts related to Edward III in 1328–9. A common idea that the name strawberry is derived from the habit of putting straw under the cultivated plants when the fruit is ripening is incorrect, although useful in practice, as the name is older than the custom. Yet another source suggests the name refers to the tiny strawlike seeds (achenes) found on the fruit.

Deliciously sweet and fragrant, the wild strawberry was a favourite woodland fruit, available to everyone; the strawberries were sold in the streets of London, done up in pottles (coneshaped straw baskets), carried on long poles and 'cried':

Rare ripe strawberries Hautboys, sixpence a pottle.

Full to the bottom, hautboys.
Strawberries and Cream are charming and sweet
Mix them and try how delightful they eat.

The strawberry plant is the birthday flower for
13 May. In the language of the flowers strawberry blossom means, 'Be on the alert', and
signifies innocence. The fruit symbolizes
esteem, love and perfection. In the Christian tradition the plant
with flower and the fruit is a symbol of the good fruits of the Holy
Spirit; the strawberry leaf represents the Trinity. The fruit is an
emblem of the Virgin Mary and John the Baptist and on his feast
day superstition decreed that the mothers of children who had died
in infancy were not supposed to eat the fruit for fear that the Virgin
Mary, deprived of her favourite fruit, would not allow the children
to enter heaven. Because it is cool and dry when green and moist
when ripe, it is an attribute of pagan love goddesses; in Norse
mythology it is sacred to Frigg, principal wife of Odin, goddess of
the clouds in the sky and of married love, who concealed dead
children in strawberry leaves and smuggled them in the clouds to
heaven. In Browne's *Pastorals* a centuries old custom is recalled
when lovers used the strawberry as a love token:

> *Making of them a bracelet on a bent [grass]*
> *Which for a favour to this swain they sent.*

Formerly a strawberry birthmark was thought to be a sign of
royalty. However, in Britain the plant does have connections with
nobility as eight strawberry leaves are incorporated into ducal
coronets and four for a marquis, and in the coat of arms of Simon,
Lord Fraser of Lovat during the reign of the Holy Roman Emperor
Charles II, the Bald (823–7), five strawberry flowers are arranged in
the form of a St Andrew's cross.

SUNFLOWER

And sunflowers planted for their gilded show,
That scale the lattice windows ere they blow,
Then sweet to habitants within the sheds,
Peep through the diamond panes their gilded heads.
John Clare *The Shepherd's Calendar*

COMMON SUNFLOWER (*Helianthus annus*) The generic name is derived from two Greek words; *helios*, 'sun', and *anthos*, 'flower'. The common name is so called from the likeness of the plant to a child's colourful painting of the radiant beams of the sun and not as was earlier believed that the flower follows the course of the sun, as expressed by Thomas Moore:

As the sunflower turns to her god when he sets
The same look which she turned when he rose.

One glance at a field of sunflowers, which is a rare sight in England, reveals they face every way indiscriminately. One fable suggested the flower eventually twisted its head right off!

The various names given to this handsome annual reflect its origins – marigold of Peru, **corona solis**, *Sola Indianus* and *chrysanthemum peruvianum* – for it is a native of Peru and Mexico and was introduced into this country in the sixteenth century. In Peru it was much revered by the Incas and the outline of the flower can be traced in the sculptures of the ancient temples. It was also woven in gold and worn by priestesses and virgins who were crowned with sunflowers and carried them in their hands; sunflower seeds are a fertility symbol and were eaten during their religious rites. The destructive Spanish conquerors, who were eventually to destroy the entire royal family of this creative race in the name of the Roman Catholic Church, also found detailed representations of the flower made in pure gold, on ornaments and jewellery and forming the head of ceremonial standards.

The arrival of such an unusual plant from what was termed the New World caused much comment and was variously described as 'Hearbe of the Sunne', that 'it was greater than a greate Platter or Dishe, the whiche hath divers coulers . . . it showeth marvelous faire in Gardens' and 'when the plant groweth to maturitie, the floures fall away, in place whereof appeareth the seed . . . set as though a cunning workman had of purpose placed them in very good order, much like the honeycombs of Bees'. The growth of the vast stalk and the expansion of the flower must have astounded those who first raised it from seed – gardener's tall stories soon followed.

The blooming of the sunflower is recorded in *An Early Calendar of English Flowers*:

> *And yet anon, the full Sunflower blew,*
> *And became a starre for Bartholomew.*

The feast of St Bartholomew is celebrated on 24 August. The flower is also a Christian symbol of religious obedience, as it was thought to face the sun (Christ) all day. It is an attribute of the Virgin Mary and Saint Ethelreda, also Daphne and Mithra.

Sunflower is the birthday flower for 30 June, symbolizing adoration, affection, constancy, false riches, glory, gratitude and infatuation. The dwarf sunflower signifies adoration and in the language of the flowers, 'your devoted admirer'.

SWEET PEA

Here are sweet peas on tip toe for a flight
With wings of gently flush o'er delicate white
And taper fingers catching at all things,
To bind them all about with tiny rings.
John Keats 'A Posy'

SWEET PEA (*Lathyrus odoratus*) *Lathyros* is an old Greek name for *L. sativus*, possibly originally from *1a*, 'very', and *thouros*, 'impetuous', alluding to the use of one of the peas in ancient medicine, and given by the philosopher Theophrastus who died aged 107, 'lamenting the shortness of life'. The sweet pea is a Sicilian wild flower which was first recorded by Father Franciscus Cupani, who described it in his *Hortus Catholicus* which was published in 1697; however, it was not until 1699 that he sent seeds to Dr Robert Uvedale of Enfield, a collector of unusual plants and one of the first garden-lovers in England to have a number of hothouses. At that time it was described as having two irregular blooms with maroon-coloured wings and a blue or purple standard. Although an illustration appeared in the *Twelve Months of Flowers* in 1730, sweet peas had been recommended by Thomas Fairchild for London gardens some years earlier when he wrote of them: 'the sweet-scented Pea makes a beautiful Plant, having Spikes of Flowers of a red and blue Colour. The Scent is somewhat like Honey and a little tending to Orange-flower Smell.' By 1754 the choice of colours had increased, as James Justice spoke of 'purple, white, and Painted Lady varieties, the last less sweetly scented than the former'.

The real pioneer of the modern sweet pea was Henry Eckford, who began to specialize in about 1870 and was so successful that by the time of the great Bi-Centenary Sweet Pea Exhibition at the Crystal Palace in 1900, of the 264 varieties exhibited 115 were of his raising; having greatly improved the shape and colour range he also increased the number of blooms on each stem from two to four.

The National Sweet Pea Society was formed the following year, which was also memorable in the history of the plant as Silas Cole, gardener to Earl Spencer at Althorp Park in Northamptonshire, caused a sensation when he exhibited a variety called Lady Spencer, the first of the waved sweet peas. Further experiments were carried out at different nurseries and the waved sweet peas were established, but by 1911 a cautionary note was sounded by a specialist: 'there is a point in development in this direction where beauty ends and vulgarity begins'. Nevertheless this was the fragrant flower *par excellence* of the Edwardian era and no dinner table, wedding or social occasion was complete without it.

It is still popular today, decorating garden and house walls, spiralling up bamboo canes in orderly lines and forming colourful wigwams and, as William Cowper noted in 'The Garden':

Some more aspiring catch the neighbour shrub
With clasping tendrils, and invest his branch,
Else unadorned, with many a gay festoon
And fragrant chaplet, recompensing well
The strength they borrow with the grace they lend.

Sweet pea is the birthday flower for 1 February and symbolizes delicacy and departure. In the language of the flowers, 'Remember me'.

SWEET WILLIAM

Sweet William small has form and aspect bright,
Like that sweet flower [pink] that yields great Jove delig[ht]
Had he majestic bulk he'd now be styled
Jove's flower, and, if my skill is not beguiled,
He was Jove's flower when Jove was but a child.
Abraham Cowley 'The Garden'

SWEET WILLIAM (*Dianthus barbatus*) The generic name signifies
Jove's flower or divine flower, from the Greek *dios*, 'divine' and *anthos*,
'flower'. Dianthus was the name given to the genus by Theophrastus in
the fourth century BC; the plants of this order are more numerous in
colder climates, with sweet scents and bright colours and markings around
the entrance to the honey supply making them most attractive for
pollination by butterflies and moths. *Barbatus* is the Latin for 'bearded'.

Take him with many flowers on one conferred
He's worthy Jove, e'en now he has a beard.

Narrow-leaved varieties of this delightful cottage-garden plant which
Gerard suggested were used to 'decke up gardens and the bosomes of the
beautiful' are called in old books sweet johns and the broad-leaved, sweet
williams. It was also known as bearded pink, velvet williams, Jove's
flower, bloomy-downs, tolmeiners and London tufts.

There is a tradition that the name refers to William the Conqueror,
but it is more probable that it was Sweet Saint William after St William

of Acquitaine, a soldier of Charlemagne's, who helped to chase the Saracens from Languedoc. He died in 812 having renounced the world four years earlier.

Sweet William is the birthday flower for 15 May, symbolizing craftiness, gallantry and treachery. In the language of the flowers it means, 'Grant me one smile'.

A historical link connects the flower with the Battle of Culloden in 1745 when the Jacobites, who were the supporters of the right of James II and his descendants to the throne of Great Britain and Ireland, were defeated by a vastly superior English army led by William, Duke of Cumberland. The ill-trained and weary remnants of the Scottish clans had made their last stand on moorland near Inverness. There was much rejoicing in England when the news of the victory reached London and an unknown poet connected this pretty flower with the Duke, who was soon to become known as the Bloody Butcher for his barbarities in suppressing the rebellion of the Young Pretender.

> *The pride of France is the lily white*
> *The rose in June is Jacobite*
> *The prickly thistle of the Scot*
> *Is northern knighthood's badge and lot;*
> *But since the Duke's victorious blows*
> *The lily, thistle and the rose*
> *All droop and fade, all die away;*
> *Sweet William only rules the day,*
> *No plant with brighter lustre grows,*
> *Except the laurel on his brow.*

Naturally when the Scots heard of this floral tribute they named one of their most obnoxious plants – stinking Billy!

TANSY

And where I often, when a child, for hours
Tried through the pales to get the tempting
*   flowers*
As lady's laces, everlasting peas,
True-Lovers-Lies-Bleeding, with the hearts-
*   at-ease,*
And golden rods, and tansy running high,
That o'er the pale tops smiled on passers-by.
J. Hulme 'Favourite Flowers'

TANSY (*Tanacetum vulgare*) The generic name is a form of medieval Latin, *tanazeta*, once regarded as a specific for intestinal worms. The common name is probably derived from the Greek, *athanaton*, 'immortal', either because it lasts so long in flower or because it was used to preserve dead bodies. Another name for the plant is *athanasia*, Greek for 'immortality', and according to one source tansy is an abbreviation of that name. It is also known as golden buttons, no doubt in reference to the small, round, flat yellow flowers which grow in saucer-shaped clusters on stems two to three feet in height above its feathery foliage, which unfortunately has a slightly disagreeable odour, not unlike camphor, although the wild tansy is more fragrant. Nevertheless it is often naturalized in our gardens for ornamental reasons and adds a tall splash of colour to the herb garden. It is mentioned in *The Muses' Elysium*:

Some camomile doth not amiss
With savory and some tansy.

Tansy is the birthday flower for 23 February, symbolizing courage and resistance. In the language of the flowers it means 'I declare against you'.

The plant was dedicated to St Athanasia and, later, the Virgin Mary. It is connected with some interesting old customs which were observed at Easter, one of which involved the archbishops and bishops playing handball with the men of the congregation, with a tansy cake the reward for the victorious team. The cakes were made from the young leaves of the plant, mixed with eggs, and were thought to purify the body after the fasting period of Lent. In time this custom became a symbol of Easter Day, in remembrance of the bitter herbs eaten by the Jews at the Feast of the Passover.

Coles (1656) says the origin of eating it in the spring is because tansy is very wholesome after the salt fish consumed during Lent, and counteracts the ill effects which the 'moist cold constitution of winter has made on people . . . some people take it for a matter of superstition to do so'. Tansy tea was very popular too, and the juice of the plant was used to flavour what has been described as a nauseating dish – tansy pudding.

> On Easter day, be the pudding seen
> To which the tansy lends her sober green.

Fresh meat was rubbed over with the tansy juice to act as a fly repellent and was said not to impair the flavour. Bundles of fresh elder and tansy laid on the windowsills and hung in the pantries were used to deter insects. The Elizabethans too favoured the herb and used it in their bedding.

TOADFLAX

And thou, Linaria, mingle in my wreath
Thy golden dragons; for though perfumed breath
Escapes not from thy yellow petals, yet
Glad thoughts bring'st thou of hedgerows foliage,
     wet
With tears and dew.
Anne Pratt 'Toadflax'

COMMON TOADFLAX (*Linaria vulgaris*) The Latin name was given because of the likeness of the plant to flax, *linum*, before flowering in early summer. The unusual name toadflax originated in the supposed resemblance of the flowers to small toads, or at least the likeness of the mouth of the flower to the wide mouth of a toad. One source, however, suggests it's because 'toads will sometimes shelter themselves under the branches of it'.

The numerous country names of the plant often reflect its colour, such as butter and eggs, the pale yellow part of the flower suggesting the former and the orange part the yolk of an egg, also eggs and bacon and churnstaff, whilst the shape of the flower confirms regional differences in an animal likeness – lion's mouth, doggies, calf's snout, monkey flower and wild snapdragon. Among the many old local names given to the plant is gallwort, on account of its bitterness, one old writer affirming that it received the name because an infusion of the leaves was used 'against the flowing of the gall in cattell'. Culpepper on the other hand wrote: 'In Sussex we call it gallwort, and lay it on our chickens water to cure them of the gall; it relieves them when they are dropping.' John Gerard described this attractive plant 'as being in shew a most glorious and goodly flower, but at the nose most lothsomly stinking'. When fresh it does have a slightly disagreeable odour which for the most part disappears when it is dry. However, John Grigson warned not to let what he called 'that devil of a yellow toadflax' into our gardens, adding 'with entire justice the Americans call it impudent lawyer, and also (from the dirty ochre of its creeping roots?) dead men's bones'.

Country people used the juice of the toadflax mixed with milk in an open dish as a means of attracting flies: the 'sweet flavour proves to them poison', and the flowers infused in milk, placed where flies were troublesome, acted as a deterrent. Because the leaves contain an acrid juice it is untouched by cattle.

The whole herb was gathered just as it was coming into flower and used either fresh or dried. Herbalists prescribed a cooling ointment made from it: a fresh plant was chopped and fried in lard until it was crisp, then strained, and the resulting fine green ointment was used to treat sores, piles, ulcers and skin complaints generally. The whole plant was also used in the form of a poultice to treat haemorrhoids. The juice of the toadflax or the distilled water from the herb was a remedy for inflammation of the eyes and for cleaning ulcerous wounds. As the toadflax is a diuretic it was highly recommended in the treatment of jaundice, liver, skin diseases and dropsy. The flowers yield a yellow dye.

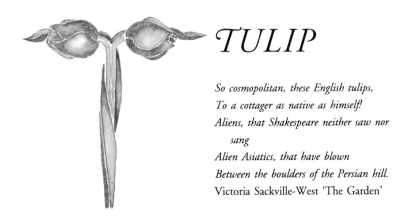

TULIP

So cosmopolitan, these English tulips,
To a cottager as native as himself!
Aliens, that Shakespeare neither saw nor
*   sang*
Alien Asiatics, that have blown
Between the boulders of the Persian hill.
Victoria Sackville-West 'The Garden'

TULIP (*Tulipa gesneriana*) *Tulipa* is the Latin version of the Persian word for 'turban'. It was the flower of the Turkish court, where it was first cultivated as a garden flower probably about the beginning of the sixteenth century. A manuscript written in about 1730 by the Grand Vizier Ilibrahim Pasha mentions 1,323 varieties. The tulip was seen growing in 1554 by the European Ambassador to Suleiman the Magnificent who subsequently took bulbs and seeds back to Vienna. *Tulipa gesneriana* was named after the Dutch botanist Conrad von Gesner who saw the flowers growing in Augsberg in 1559 and published a description of them. It is a hybrid and the principal ancestor of the garden tulips today, and it was introduced to England in about 1578. In 1582 Thomas Hakluyt wrote: 'Within these four yeares there have been brought into England from Vienna in Austria divers kinds of flowers called Tulipas, and these and others procured thither a little before from Constantinople by an excellent man called M Carolus Clusius.' John Rea, author of *Flora, Ceres and Pomona* (1665), listed some 174 varieties and mentioned others 'which to enumerate would fill a considerable volume' and also commented that the 'striped, feathered, garded or variously marbled' were the most popular, many with delightful names too.

Then comes the tulip race, where beauty plays
Her ideal freaks; from family diffus'd,
To family, as flies the father dust,
The varied colours run.

According to Alice M. Coates in *Flowers and Their Histories* 'a number of tulip species grow wild in various parts of Europe, it is thought that they are not native there, but are descended from bulbs imported long ago from Asia Minor – perhaps by the Crusaders'.

It is difficult to comprehend the fortunes that were made and lost in the European bulb trade during the seventeenth century. People called it tulip mania as single bulbs fetched thousands of pounds, and precious varieties were stolen, or worse – eaten.

In the language of the flowers the tulip symbolizes eloquence, eternal separation, fame, extravagance, oratory and spring. A red tulip is the birthday flower for 7 June, symbolizing ardent love; a variegated tulip is the birthday flower for 8 June and in the language of the flowers means 'Your eyes are beautiful'. A yellow tulip signifies hopeless love. In the Christian tradition the tulip is the emblem of Christ, symbolic of the chalice.

Tulip bulbs preserved in sugar were eaten as a sweetmeat having a similar taste 'almost as pleasant as the Eringus rootes' wrote one enthusiast. The bulbs were also believed to be an aphrodisiac, and a writer of the time commented cautiously, 'I cannot say either from my selfe, not having eaten many . . .'

VALERIAN

And by the dusty road
Bedstraw and Mullien tall,
With red Valerian
And Toadflax on the wall.
Robert Bridges 'The Idle Flowers'

COMMON VALERIAN (*Valeriana officinalis*) The generic and common names are from Latin *valere*, 'to be healthy', on account of its medicinal virtues. Older writers attribute the name to Valerius, a Roman physician, who, it is said, first used the plant as a medicinal herb. Country names for valerian, of which there are several species, include setwall, all-heal, Bovis and soldiers, capon's tail, phu and amantilla (a fourteenth-century name). A recipe from that time suggests 'Men who begin to fight and you wish to stop them, give to them the juice of Amantilla id est Valeriana and peace will be made immediately'.

Valerian is the birthday flower for 16 March and symbolizes a good disposition. Astrologically the plant is under the dominion of Mercury.

The rich dark green leaves and the crowning mass of the pale pink flowers of this tall plant compensate for a slightly disagreeable odour which cats are said to delight in, and which accounts for the name phu. A North Country saying quoted by the herbalist John Gerard advises:

They that will have their heale
Must put Setwall in their keale.

'The dry root', he continued, 'is put into counterpoysons and medicines preservatives against the pestilence: whereupon it hath been had (and is to

this day among the poore people of our North-
erne parts) in such veneration amongst them,
that no broths, pottage or physicall meats are
worth any thing, if Setwall were not at an
end.' Valerian has been used for many
centuries; one foreign species, which has a
distinctive fragrance, dried, was used in the
preparation of the aromatic spikenard mentioned
in the Scriptures. It was so prized by the Romans
that Horace promised Virgo several dozen containers of wine for
one box – they used to anoint their guests with it, use it as a
perfume and as a medicine for hysteria and epilepsy. Medieval
herbalists recommended the dry root as a specific for cramp. The
roots were collected in the autumn, sliced, and dried in kilns or
ovens giving off a 'disagreeable odour'.

> *Valerian then he crops, and purposely doth stamp,*
> *To apply into the place that's haled with cramp.*

In the Middle Ages the roots were also used to perfume linen
clothing.

Although the plant has long been included in the *British
Pharmacopoeia*, an article in a medical journal in 1928 suggested
that it 'was perhaps the earliest method of treating neuroses'. During
the twentieth century, valerian has been used to treat nervous
headaches, epilepsy and, as a medical placebo, hypochondria. A tea
brewed from the dry roots is alleged to be one of the strongest
herbal sedatives. Nevertheless, valerian was also used as an
aphrodisiac and it was said that those who wore valerian would
never lack lovers.

VIOLET

The violet in her greenwood bower,
Where birchen bows with hazel mingle,
May boast itself the fairest flower
In glen or copse or forest dingle.
Sir Walter Scott 'The Violet'

V I O L E T (*Viola*) The generic name is the Latin word for various sweet-scented flowers, especially the violet, derived from the same source as the Greek *ion*, from Io, a daughter of Inachus, king of Argos, beloved by Zeus. To save Io from the jealous intrigues of Hera (Zeus' wife) the god transformed her into a white heifer:

Io, the mild shape,
Hidden by Jove's [Zeus'] fears,
Found us first i'the sward, when she
For hunger stooped in tears;
Wheresoe'r her lips she sets,
Said Jove, be breaths called violets

Greek legend however claims that the violet sprang from the blood of Aias (Roman Ajax), a man of great stature, second only to Achilles as a hero of the Trojan War, who committed suicide having slain the sheep of the Greeks in error, allegedly after a bout of jealousy when the armour of the slain Achilles was awarded to Odysseus instead of him. Violets are also said to have sprung up from the blood of Attis, a Phrygian deity of vegetation, a youth of great beauty who was changed into a fir tree by Cybele to prevent him killing himself after she discovered he had broken his vow of chastity and married the daughter of the river Sangarius. After he was slain his rebirth was celebrated every spring with song.

Astrologically the violet is under the dominion of Venus and the sign of Aries. The flower symbolizes constancy, modesty, humility, mourning, steadfastness and watchfulness. Various species and colours are assigned to different days: blue violet is the birthday flower for 11 March, symbolizing faithfulness and also love; purple violet in the language of the flowers means 'You occupy my thoughts', white violet is the birthday flower for 14 March symbolizing candour, innocence and modesty; wild violet signifies 'Love in idleness' and yellow violet, the birthday flower for 28 April, rare worth and rural happiness. In earlier times the prize of a golden violet was offered to the best versifier, indicating the esteem in which the flower was held.

Historically the flower is associated with Napoleon Bonaparte who, when banished to the island of Elba, told his friends that he would return with the violets. 'Corporal Violet' became a favourite toast of his supporters and when he did return, women assembled with bunches of violets and asked buyers the question, 'Do you like violets?' If they did not answer, 'Eh bien,' they knew the person was not a confederate. The Empress Josephine is said to have thrown a bunch of violets to Napoleon at their first meeting. Violets were also strewn on the grave of Nero by an unknown person and statues of him were 'crowned with garlands of flowers'.

Violets were used in the religious ceremony 'Creeping the Cross', celebrated on Good Friday, when priests in crimson robes, singing mournfully, carried a representation of the cross accompanied by an image of a dead person.

In more recent times it was a popular choice for a posy for young people making their annual visit home on Mothering Sunday, which gave rise to the saying: 'Go a-mothering, and find violets in the lane.'

Pliny referred to the violet's excellent properties: the odour of some of the species allegedly cured headaches and healing qualities were contained in the leaves and flowers. In the Middle Ages dried flower petals, powdered and taken in water, were used as a preventative medicine for pleurisy, epilepsy, quinsy, jaundice and headaches, and a laxative syrup made from fresh violets was prescribed for children.

WOOD SORREL

Here breathes, how frail! a puce-veined bell,
There snowy droops its crumpled hood.
With knotted roots of tinctured strings
A tender tapestry it weaves,
While folding back like soft green wings
The lappets of its cloven leaves.
Charles A. Fox 'The Wood Sorrel'

WOOD SORREL (*Oxalis acetosella*) The generic name is Greek for the plant: it comes from Greek, *oxys*, 'sharp or acid', referring to the acidity of the leaves; *acetosella* is from Latin *acetum*, 'vinegar'. Wood sorrel has delicate triple leaves often lined with purple and fragile white flowers, flourishing in deepest woodland shade. It has many country names such as wood sour, fairy bells, sour trefoil, three-leaved grass, cuckoo-sorrel and alleluia-flower with variations according to different writers. Gerard calls it alleluya or cuckoo meate, because, he says, 'either the cuckoo feedeth thereon, or by reason when it springeth foorth and flowreth the alleluya is sung in the churches'; it blooms between Easter and Whitsuntide. Cuckoo-sorrel originates from the idea that the bird used the plant to clear its voice, and fairy bells, a Welsh name, from the charming belief that the merry peal of its bells called the elves to moonlight revelry. Older writers have claimed it to be the true shamrock of St Patrick – it is in bloom on his feast day 17 March.

Heart shaped and triply folded, and its root
Creeping like beaded coral.

Wood sorrel was an old druidic emblem in Ireland, a lucky symbol associated with the ancient Celtic sun wheel long before AD 432, when the saint arrived to teach Christianity. He is said to have used the familiar leaf to explain the Holy Trinity to the Irish people. Nowadays a tiny type of clover is generally accepted as the 'true shamrock'.

Astrologically wood sorrel is assigned to Venus. In the language of the flowers it signifies joy and maternal tenderness. The plant with its delicate flowers is frequently depicted in ecclesiastical paintings and wood carvings. John Ruskin, the nineteenth-century author and art critic, wrote: 'The triple leaf of this plant and the white flower stained purple probably gave it a strange typical interest among Christian painters.' He also noted that Italian painters favoured the flower: 'Fra Angelico's use of the *Oxalis acetosella* is as faithful in representation as touching in feeling.'

The leaves of the plant have a pleasant acid taste and have been used from time immemorial as a spring salad herb. They also provided the basis of a green sauce taken with fish. Gerard wrote of it 'Greene Sauce is good for them that have sicke and feeble stomaches . . . and of all Sauces, Sorrel is best, not only in virtue, but also in pleasantness of his taste'. Syrups and sauces were used to treat mouth ulcers and sore throats and as an appetizer for cleansing the blood:

> *Here cooling sorrel, that againe*
> *We use in hot diseases*

wrote Michael Drayton. The Greek and Roman physicians, however, used the plant for kidney complaints.

WOODY NIGHTSHADE

And hedgerows, bordering unfrequented lanes
Bower'd with wild rose, and the clasping woodbine,
Where purple tassels of the tangling vetch
With bittersweet and bryony inweave.
Charlotte Smith 'Beachy Head'

WOODY NIGHTSHADE (*Solanum dulcamara*) *Solanum* was the name given by Pliny, the Roman naturalist, to one of the nightshades, possibly derived from Latin *solamen*, 'solace', from its medicinal virtues. The majority of the nightshade family have narcotic properties and are some of the most poisonous of our native plants. *Dulcamara* literally means 'bittersweet' in Latin; it is an old country name by which the plant is still known, given because the stem and root, if chewed, first taste bitter and then sweet. It was named woody nightshade by old herbalists, to distinguish it from the deadly nightshade, *Atropa belladonna*; the leaves do bear a resemblance and the flowers are purple, though totally distinct in shape, and both have berries although they are red in this plant, as opposed to black.

Country names for the herb are felonwort, scarlet berry, violet bloom, felonwood and dulcamara; felon was an old name for a whitlow and one old writer recommended that 'the Berries of Bittersweet stamped with rusty Bacon, applied to the Joynts of the Finger that is troubled with a Felon hath been found by divers country people who are most subject thereto to be very successful for curing the same'.

Woody nightshade is the birthday flower for 19 July and in the language of the flowers bears the sentiment truth. Astrologically it is assigned to Mercury.

In the days of a strong belief in witchcraft, shepherds would hang the plant round the necks of sheep which they suspected of being under the evil eye.

Older physicians valued the herb and applied it to many uses in medicine and surgery. Linnaeus, who at first had an aversion to it, later admitted it was an excellent remedy for fever, rheumatism and inflammatory diseases. In fact it has been suggested there were few complaints for which it has not been at some time recommended. Gerard's approach to the herb was more dramatic: 'The juice is good for those that have fallen from high places, and have thereby been bruised or beaten, for it is thought to dissolve blood congealed or cluttered anywhere in the intrals and to heale the hurt places.' Culpepper warned of the dangers of confusing it with the deadly nightshade – 'if you know it not, you may then let them both alone'. He did suggest, however, that the juice mixed with a little vinegar as a remedy for a sore mouth and throat and the juice and berries, with oil of roses with a little vinegar, beaten in a mortar, for inflammation in the eyes.

More recently it was the dried young branches from our indigenous plants when they have shed their leaves that were the parts used and were recommended as late as 1907 in the *British Pharmacopoeia*.

YARROW

Thou pretty herb of Venus-tree,
Thy true name is Yarrow;
Now who my bosom friends must be,
Pray tell thou me tomorrow.
Old Rhyme 'Venus-tree'

YARROW (*Achillea millefolium*) The generic name has its root in the Greek legend which tells how Achilles, who had learned the art of healing by the use of herbs from Chiron, the wisest of all the Centaurs, saved the life of an injured king; when the Greeks invaded Troy, Telephus, King of the Mysians, was wounded with a spear. Achilles scraped some rust from his own spear, and as the filings fell to the ground the plant sprang up and was used to effect a cure. The specific name means 'thousand-leaved' in Latin and the common one, yarrow, is a corruption of Old English *gearwe* alluding to the many indentations of the leaf.

The majority of the country names, however, refer to the plant's use in herbal remedies – soldier's woundwort, nosebleed and sneezewort (it was formerly used as a snuff), and on account of the pungency of the foliage, old man's pepper. It is also known as green arrow and thousand-leaf.

Yarrow is the birthday flower for 16 January and symbolizes heartache and cure.

The superstitious had great faith in the yarrow as a protective plant against evil spirits and it was for this reason that it was woven into the floral garlands which decorated homes and churches on Midsummer Eve. Although medieval witches were believed to favour the plant in spells and potions it was later used as a charm against them and strewn across thresholds and fastened to babies' cradles.

Girls would use the plant as a love oracle by cutting the stem crosswise – the initials of one's future husband were said to appear. As the plant was also used as a means of making one's nose bleed it was incorporated into an unusual form of love divination to test the feelings of one's lover.

> *Green 'arrow, green 'arrow, you bears a white blow*
> *If my love loves me my nose will bleed now.*

A less drastic ritual to enable one to dream of one's future spouse involved placing an ounce of yarrow in a piece of flannel under the pillow and saying the opening rhyme, to the Venus-tree. Eaten at a wedding yarrow was said to guarantee happiness for the bride and groom for the first seven years.

An ancient charm for curing a fever required a yarrow leaf to be pulled off a stem with the left hand whilst saying the sick person's name and then eating the leaf. It was generally considered to be a magic herb, acquiring the unfortunate name, Devil's nettle.

Older herbalists recommended chewing the leaves as a remedy against toothache, pushing them up the nose to cause a nosebleed which would then ease the 'pain of megrim' and bathing the head with a decoction of the plant as it 'stayeth shedding the hair'. A tea, which was claimed to be stimulating, healing and an astringent was prescribed for kidney disorders. As recently as this century yarrow was used to treat chronic dysentery, bleeding from the lungs, excessive menstruation and colic.

INDEX